IMAGERY FROM THE COLLECTIVE
VOLUME 3

HUMAN ARCHETYPES - A VISUAL JOURNEY INTO SELF AND OTHER THROUGH THE EYES OF AI

ZHAMEESHA LLC
ATLANTIS, FL (USA)

Imagery from the Collective - Volume 3

Human Archetypes - A Visual Journey into Self and Other through the eyes of AI

ISBN 978-1-951645-31-1
First Edition, Print on Demand
This version was most recently updated 2025-02-23

Published by Zhameesha LLC
Atlantis, Florida USA
https://www.zhameesha.com

This book is a work of humility.

BISAC Subject Headings (www.bisg.org)
PSY023000 PSYCHOLOGY / Personality
ART037000 ART / Subjects & Themes / Human Figure
PHI005000 PHILOSOPHY / Movements / Humanism

12 11 10 9 8 7 6 5 4 3 2 1

WELCOME

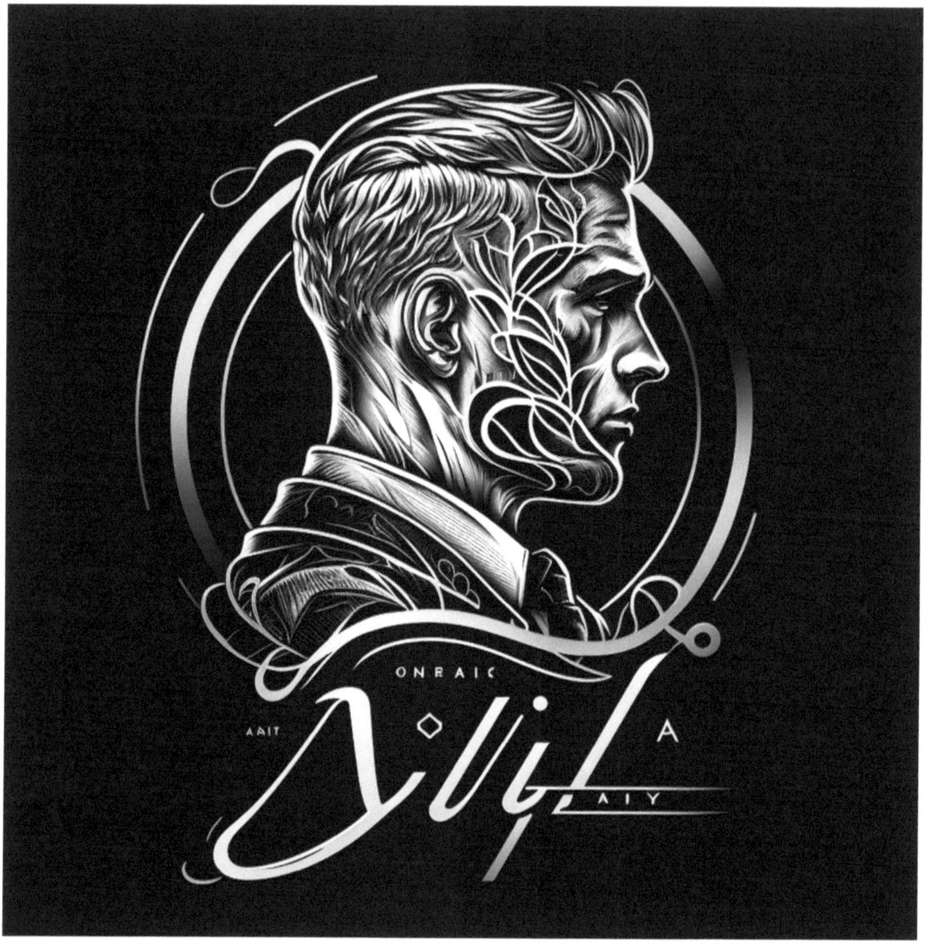

W*hat defines us as human?* Is it the stories we tell, the roles we play, or the dreams we chase? This book invites you to journey through the timeless and universal figures that inhabit our collective consciousness—the ***archetypes*** that shape who we are, how we relate, and how we see the world.

Each **archetype** presented here is a reflection of the countless lives lived, lessons learned, and emotions felt across generations. The text and visuals are born from collaboration with AI, using tools that tap into vast reservoirs of human creativity and insight. These archetypes are more than static descriptions; they are living symbols, evolving with each reader's interpretation.

As you turn these pages, we encourage you to do more than observe—engage. Reflect on how each archetype resonates with your own experiences, challenges your perceptions, or illuminates your understanding of others. Whether you see yourself in these figures or find them alien and new, they are all threads in the intricate tapestry of our shared humanity.

Welcome to this exploration of self and other, of the individual and the collective. Let this book be a mirror, a map, and a muse for your own journey.

With curiosity and wonder,
Stuart Barry Malin

The Soul of Human Being

In the context of ***Imagery from the Collective***, "**the collective**" refers to the vast and interconnected body of human knowledge, cultural symbols, archetypes, emotions, and existential inquiries that shape our shared experience.

The images in this book are not merely individual expressions but are sourced from the collective—emerging from the deep reservoirs of artistic tradition, psychological motifs, and historical narratives embedded within the vast datasets that AI has been trained on.

Just as human artists unconsciously draw upon collective memory—mythologies, literature, emotions, and philosophies—AI, too, processes and reinterprets patterns that reflect our shared human consciousness.

These images, therefore, are not created in isolation but are manifestations of something larger than any single mind. They are fragments of a broader, interconnected web of human thought and perception, filtered through the unique lens of artificial intelligence.

By engaging with these images, we are not just witnessing AI-generated art—we are gazing into the very soul of **Human Being** as represented by the collective, uncovering visual representations of ideas, emotions, and existential truths that have been shaped by humanity's long and evolving narrative.

CONTENTS

Contents

Welcome

The Archetypes

Postmatter

THE ARCHETYPES

The Abandoned Child Archetype

The Abandoned Child Archetype embodies feelings of rejection, loneliness, and a deep-seated fear of being left alone or unloved. This archetype represents individuals who have experienced abandonment, neglect, or a lack of nurturing, often during childhood, which shapes their perceptions and behaviors in adult life. Key characteristics include:

- ***Fear of Abandonment***: A persistent worry that important people in their life will leave, reject, or withdraw their love and support.
- ***Need for Approval***: Often seeks validation and reassurance from others to feel secure and loved.
- ***Sensitivity to Rejection***: May be highly attuned to any signs of disapproval or distancing, which can trigger feelings of insecurity or anxiety.
- ***People-Pleasing***: Might go to great lengths to accommodate others' needs and expectations, sometimes at the expense of their own well-being.
- ***Independence***: In some cases, may develop a strong sense of self-reliance and resilience, learning to depend on themselves rather than others.

The **Abandoned Child** is often depicted in literature, film, and cultural narratives as characters who struggle with feelings of inadequacy, insecurity, and a deep need for love and belonging. This archetype highlights the enduring impact of early experiences on an individual's emotional landscape and their journey towards healing and self-acceptance.

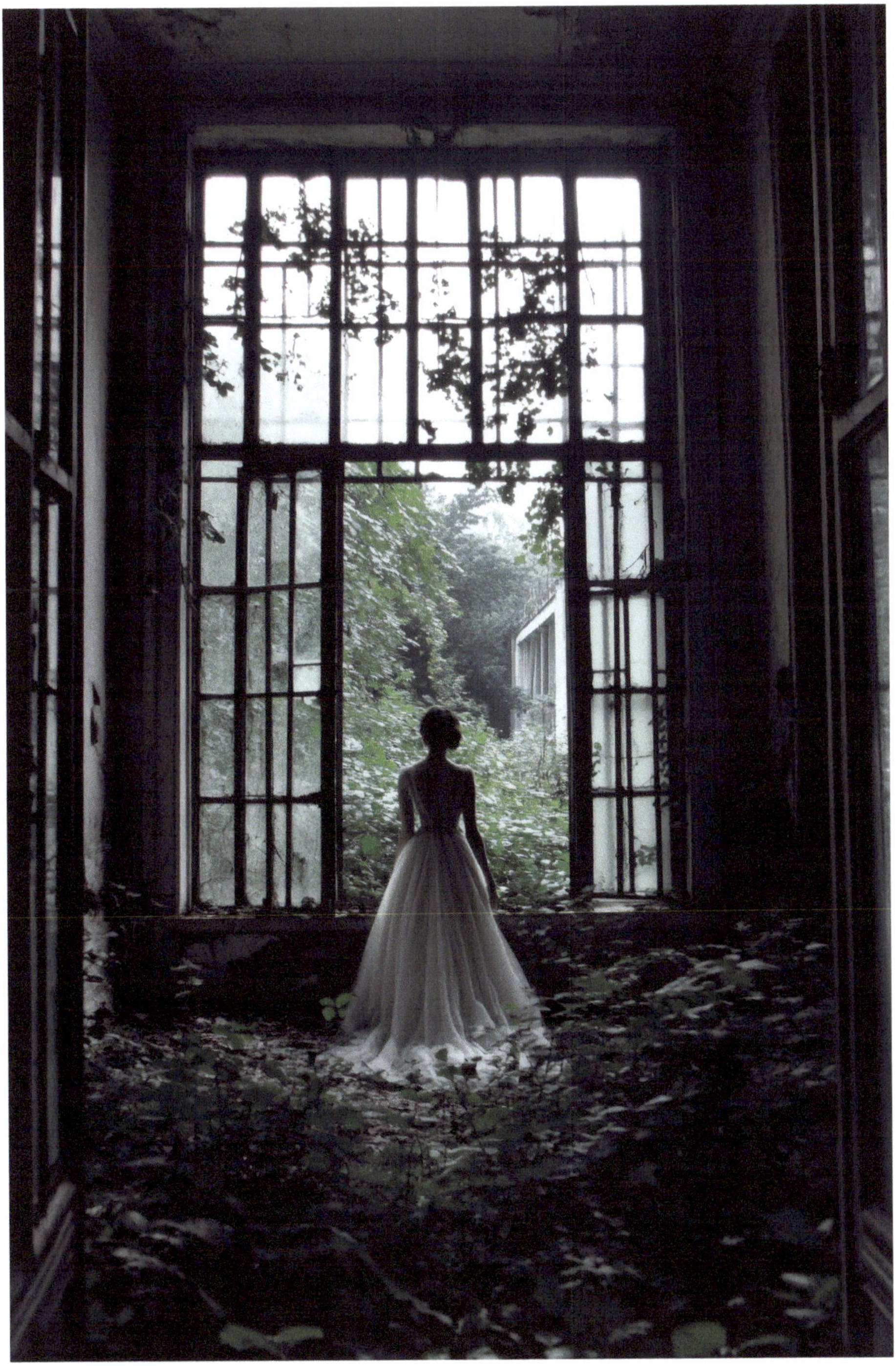

The Alien Archetype

The Alien Archetype embodies otherness, the unknown, and the sense of being a stranger or outsider. This archetype represents individuals or entities that are perceived as different, foreign, or not belonging to the familiar world, often evoking feelings of curiosity, fear, or fascination. Key characteristics include:

- ***Otherness***: Clearly distinct from the norm or the familiar, often in appearance, behavior, or origins.
- ***Mystery***: Surrounded by an aura of the unknown, incomprehensible, or enigmatic, making them difficult to understand or predict.
- ***Isolation***: Often separated or distanced from others, either by choice or due to their inherent differences.
- ***Fear/Fascination***: Can evoke strong reactions ranging from fear and distrust to intrigue and attraction, reflecting the human response to the unknown.
- ***Adaptability***: May possess the ability to assimilate, change, or evolve, allowing them to navigate and survive in unfamiliar environments.

The **Alien** is often depicted in literature, film, and popular culture as extraterrestrial beings, foreigners or strangers in a new land, and supernatural or mythical creatures that embody otherness.

This archetype highlights the human experience of encountering the unknown, the tension between belonging and otherness, and the complex emotions and reactions that arise from engaging with the unfamiliar or mysterious.

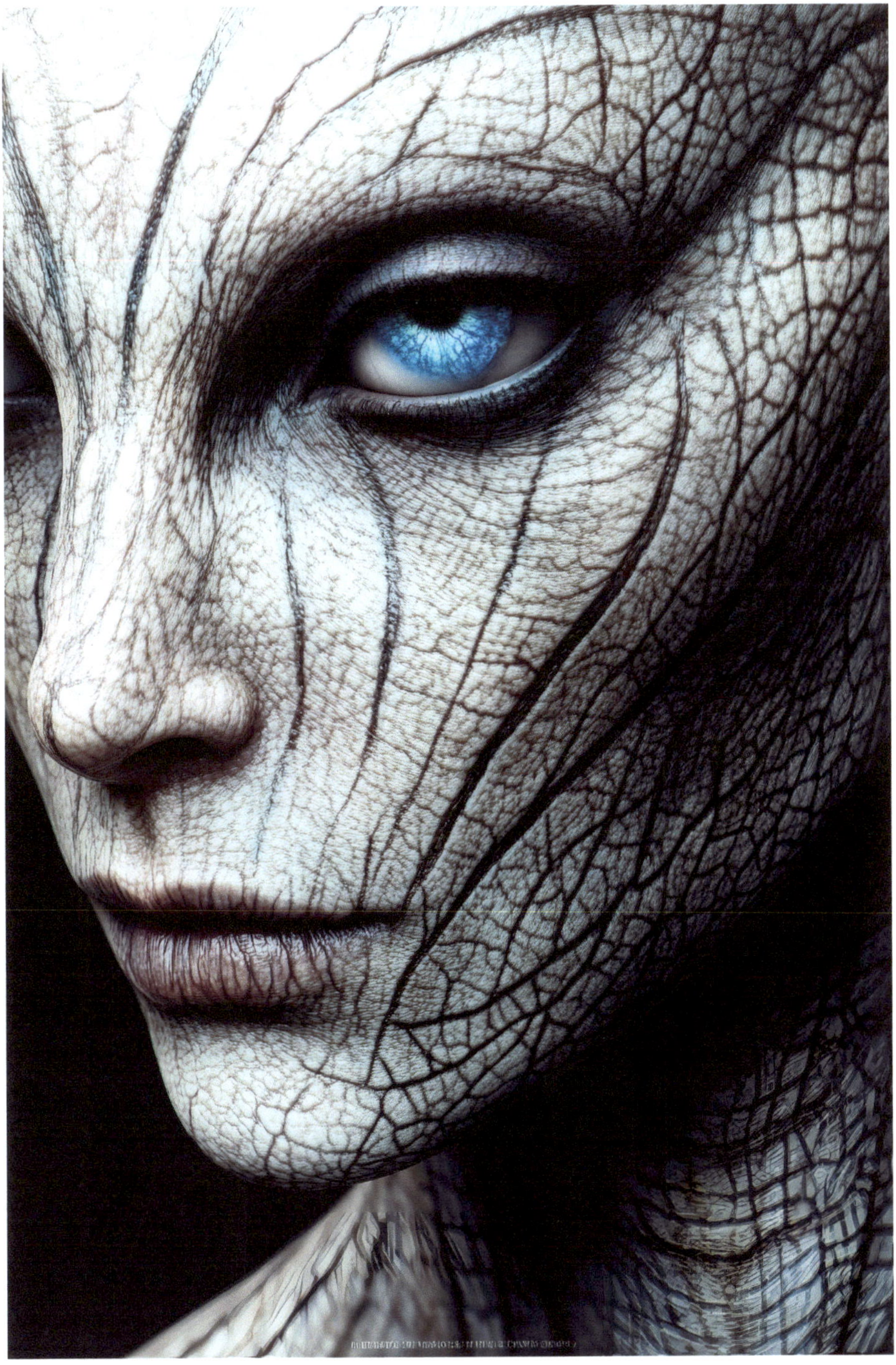

The Ancestor/Elder Archetype

The Ancestor/Elder archetype embodies wisdom, experience, and guidance passed down through generations. This archetype represents the collective knowledge, traditions, and insights of those who have come before, serving as a bridge between the past and the present. Key characteristics include:

- **Wisdom**: Deep understanding and insight gained through a lifetime of experiences.
- **Guidance**: Acts as a mentor or advisor, offering counsel and support to younger generations.
- **Tradition**: Upholds cultural practices, stories, and values, ensuring their continuation.
- **Respect**: Commands deference and admiration due to their age, experience, and role in the community.

The **Ancestor/Elder** is often depicted in stories, myths, and cultural narratives as wise old sages, tribal leaders, or revered family patriarchs and matriarchs.

Examples include characters like ***Obi-Wan Kenobi*** in Star Wars, the elderly and wise characters in many ***Native American*** stories, and historical figures known for their wisdom and guidance.

This archetype highlights the importance of learning from the past, valuing the insights of elders, and preserving cultural heritage.

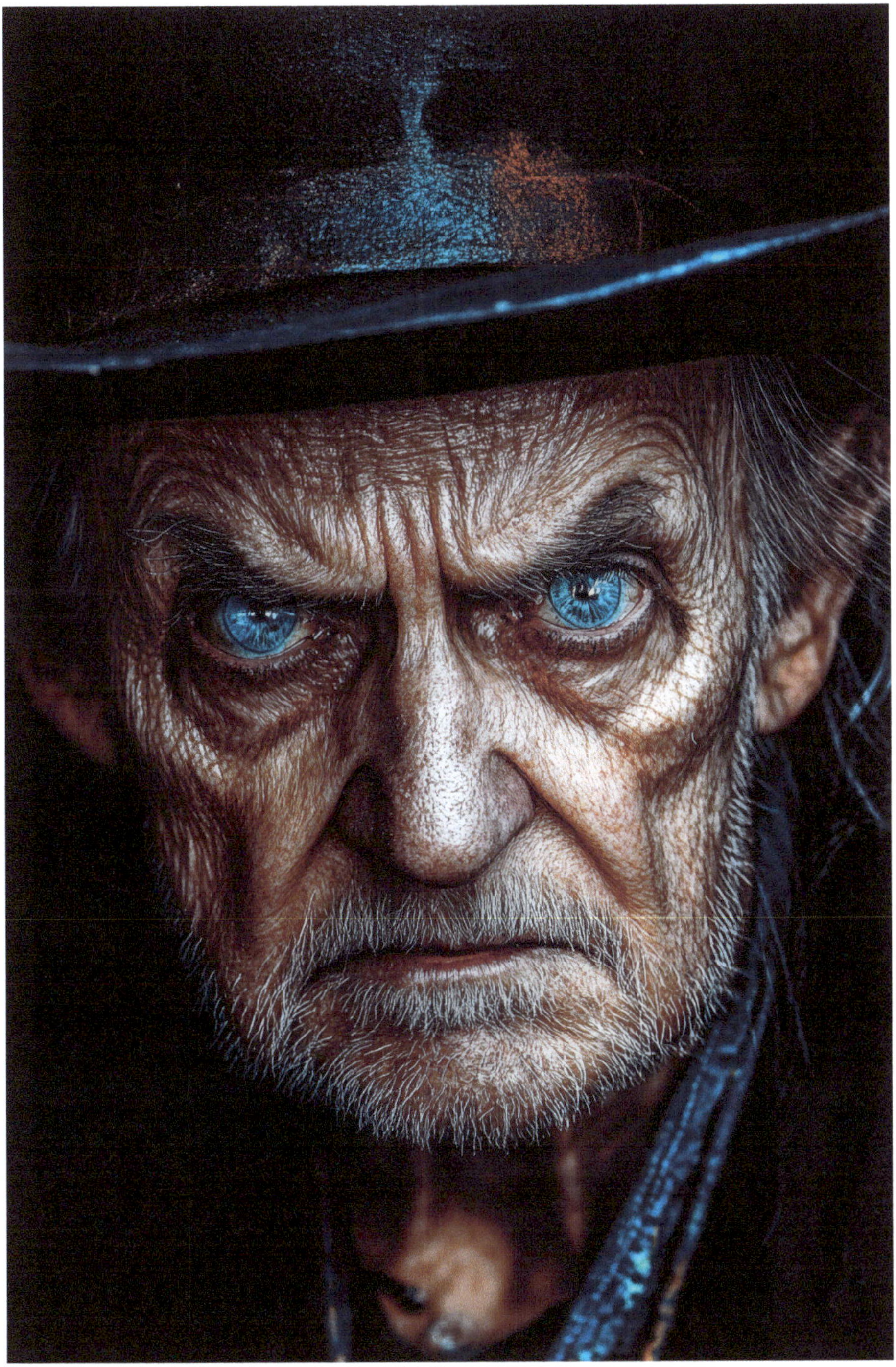

The Anima/Animus Archetypes

The Anima and Animus archetypes are concepts introduced by psychologist Carl Jung to represent the unconscious feminine side of men (Anima) and the unconscious masculine side of women (Animus). These archetypes embody the qualities and characteristics typically associated with the opposite gender, which are often repressed or underdeveloped in the individual's conscious personality.

- **The Anima** in men is often depicted as a figure that embodies emotions, intuition, creativity, and nurturing qualities. It can manifest in dreams, fantasies, or projections onto women in a man's life.
- **The Animus** in women represents logic, assertiveness, and analytical thinking. It can appear in dreams, fantasies, or projections onto men in a woman's life.

Both archetypes play a crucial role in the process of individuation, which is the journey towards psychological wholeness and self-realization.

By integrating the **Anima** or **Animus**, individuals can achieve a more balanced and complete sense of self, embracing both their masculine and feminine aspects.

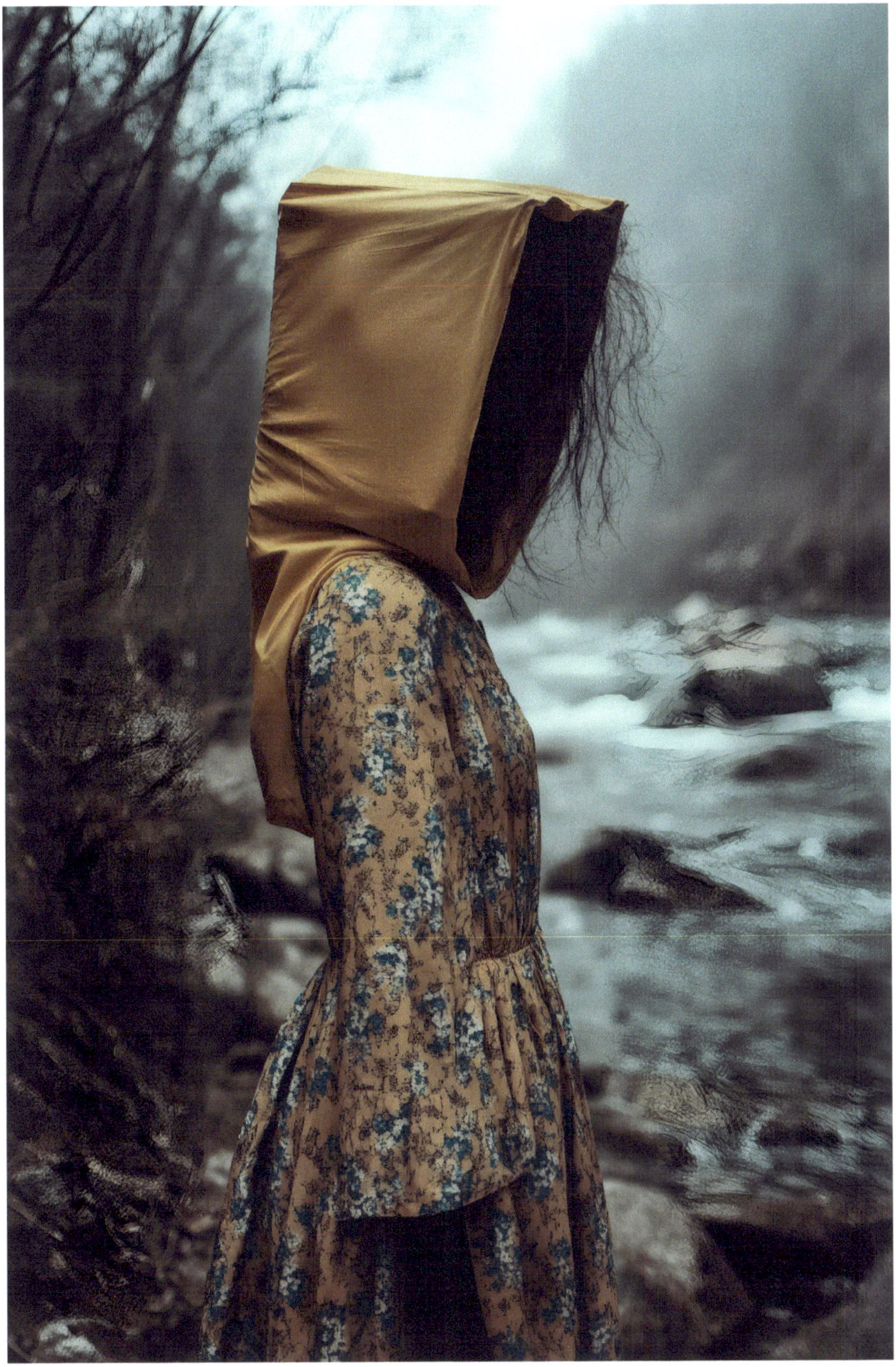

The Artist Archetype

The **Artist a**rchetype embodies creativity, self-expression, and the pursuit of beauty and meaning through artistic endeavors. This archetype represents individuals who are driven by a deep need to create, innovate, and communicate their unique vision to the world. Key characteristics include:

- ***Creativity***: A strong impulse to produce original works, whether in visual arts, music, literature, or other forms of expression.
- ***Self-Expression***: The need to communicate personal emotions, ideas, and experiences through art.
- ***Inspiration***: Often driven by a sense of higher purpose or muse, seeking to capture and convey profound insights or emotions.
- ***Non-Conformity***: May challenge conventional norms and expectations, forging new paths and pushing artistic boundaries.
- ***Sensitivity***: Acutely attuned to their surroundings, emotions, and the nuances of human experience, which informs their creative process.

The **Artist** is often depicted in stories, films, and cultural narratives as painters, musicians, writers, and other creative individuals who leave a lasting impact on the world through their work.

Examples include characters like **Vincent van Gogh**, **Frida Kahlo**, and the passionate, often tortured artists portrayed in various narratives. This archetype highlights the human desire for self-expression, the power of creativity, and the transformative impact of art on both the individual and society.

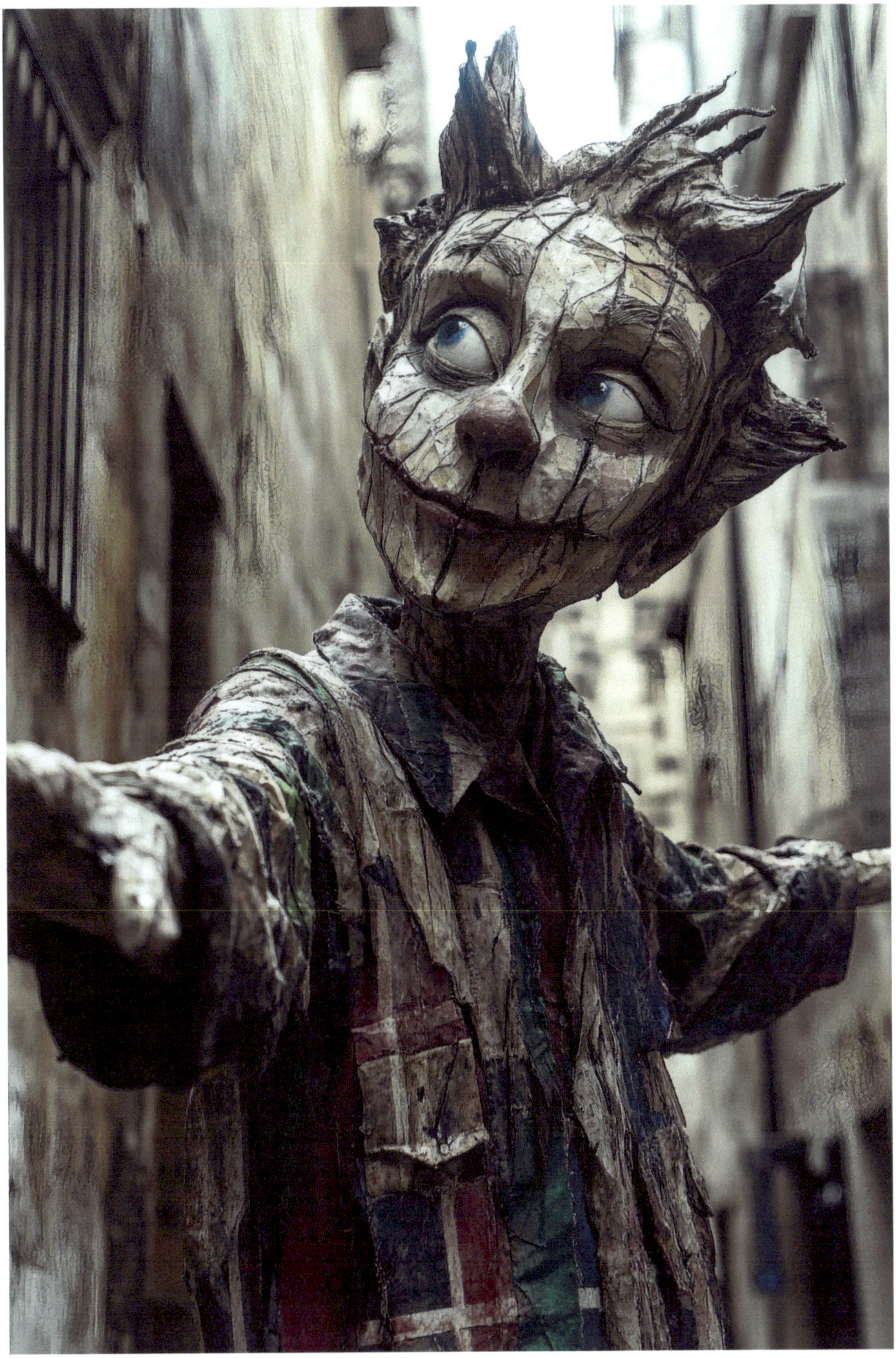

The Child Archetype

The **Child a**rchetype embodies youth, vulnerability, and the potential for growth and development. This archetype represents the early stages of life, characterized by innocence, playfulness, and a sense of wonder. Key characteristics include:

- ***Innocence***: Purity and lack of worldly experience, often coupled with a sense of naivety.
- ***Playfulness***: A joyful, imaginative, and spontaneous approach to life.
- ***Vulnerability***: Dependent on others for care and protection, with a heightened sensitivity to emotions and experiences.
- ***Potential***: The capacity for growth, learning, and development, with a future full of possibilities.
- ***Curiosity***: A strong desire to explore, discover, and understand the world.

The **Child** is often depicted in literature, film, and cultural narratives as young protagonists, orphaned or abandoned children, or characters who embody the qualities of youth and innocence.

Examples include characters like **Peter Pan**, **Oliver Twist**, and other figures who represent the joys, challenges, and complexities of childhood.

This archetype highlights the human experiences of early life, the process of maturation, and the enduring power of innocence and potential.

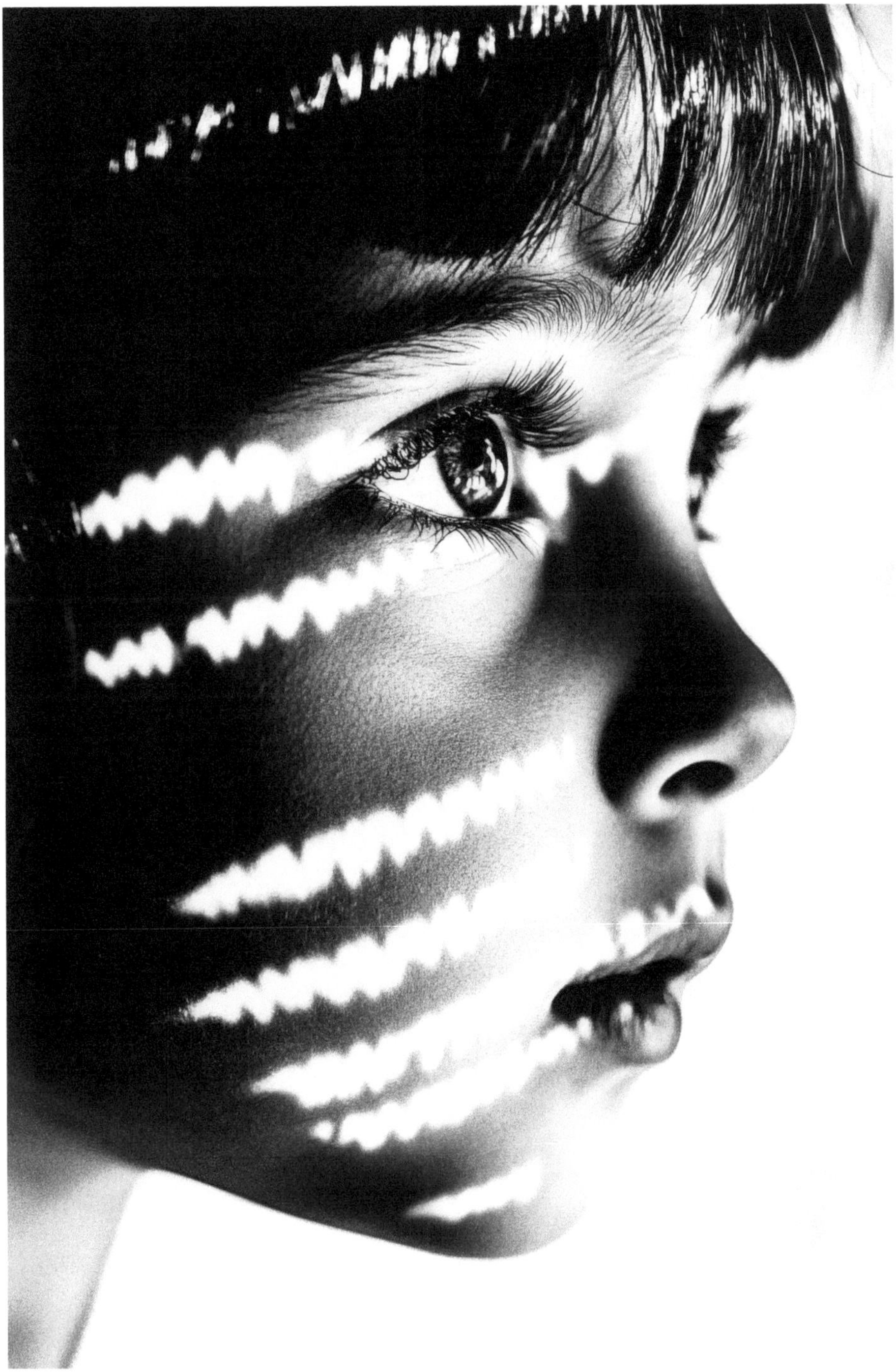

The Beacon/Lighthouse as a Symbol of Guidance

The Beacon/Lighthouse as a Symbol of Guidance represents a source of light, hope, and direction that helps individuals navigate through darkness, uncertainty, or challenging times. This symbol embodies the idea of a steady, reliable force that offers reassurance, clarity, and a sense of security to those in need. Key aspects include:

- ***Orientation***: Provides a clear, visible point of reference that helps others determine their position or find their way.
- ***Warning***: Alerts individuals to potential dangers or obstacles ahead, allowing them to make informed decisions and stay on course.
- ***Reassurance***: Offers a sense of comfort, hope, and safety, reminding others that they are not alone in their journey and that help is available.
- ***Consistency***: Remains steadfast and unwavering, serving as a dependable source of support and direction, even in the most turbulent times.
- ***Inspiration***: Encourages others to persevere, maintain their focus, and strive towards their goals, despite the challenges they may face.

The **Beacon/Lighthouse** as a symbol of guidance is often depicted in literature, art, and popular culture as a literal lighthouse, guiding ships safely to shore, a metaphorical source of light and hope, a guiding principle, ideal, or moral compass that helps individuals make decisions and live meaningful lives, a spiritual or religious symbol, representing divine guidance, salvation, or enlightenment, as seen in various faiths and traditions.

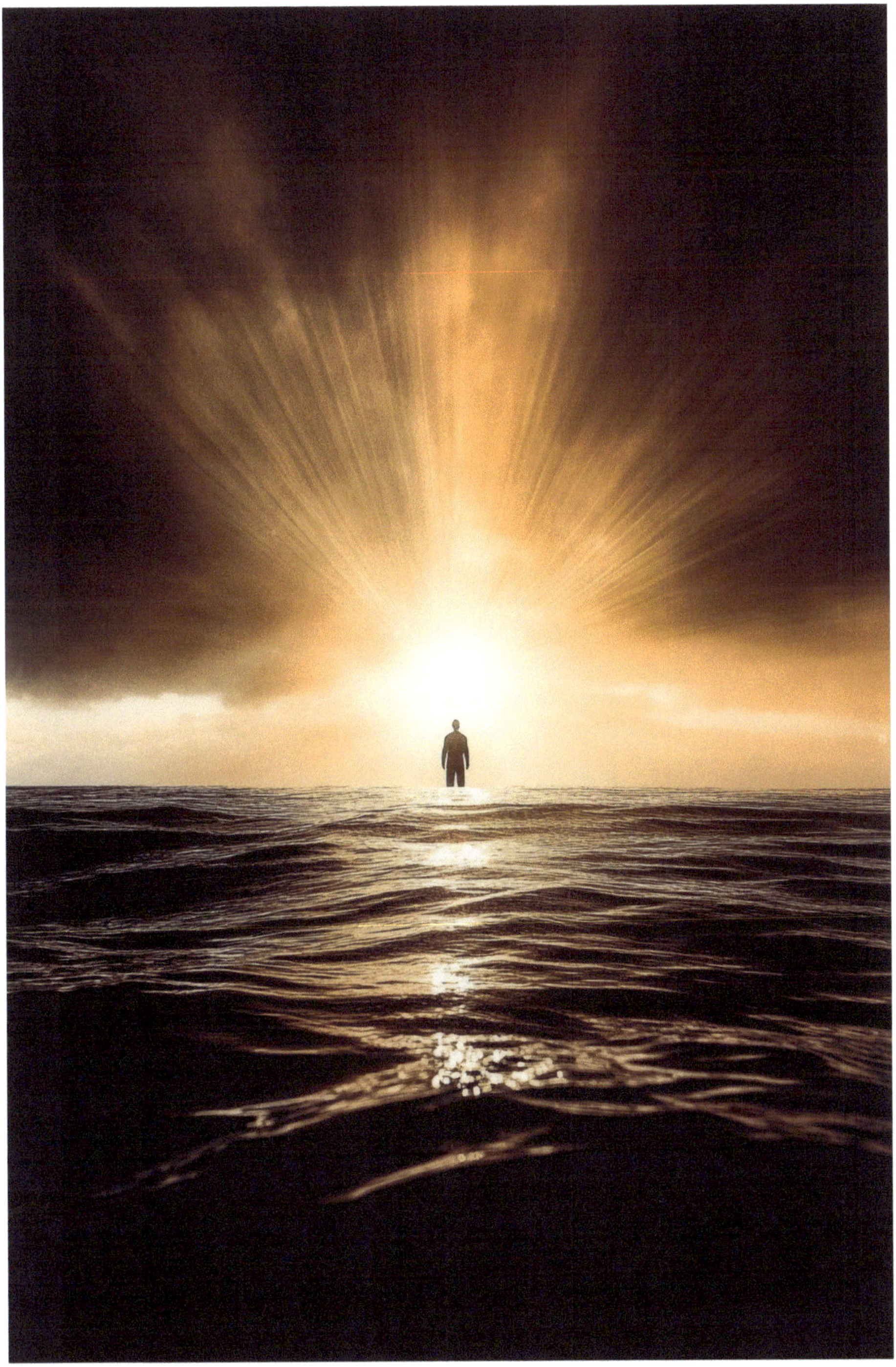

The Collective Unconscious

The Collective Unconscious is a concept introduced by Swiss psychiatrist Carl Jung. It refers to a deep, universal psychic layer shared by all humans, underlying the personal unconscious. This collective layer is not developed from personal experiences but is rather inherited and structured by archetypes—innate, universal patterns and symbols. Key aspects of **The Collective Unconscious** include:

- ***Universality***: Shared by all humans, regardless of individual experiences or cultural backgrounds.
- ***Archetypes***: Contains universal symbols, themes, and patterns that recur across different cultures and historical periods.
- ***Inherited***: Passed down through generations, much like instincts.
- ***Manifestation***: Often revealed in dreams, myths, fairy tales, and cultural narratives.

The **Collective Unconscious** influences behaviors, emotions, and perceptions, providing a framework for understanding universal human experiences and the interconnectedness of all individuals.

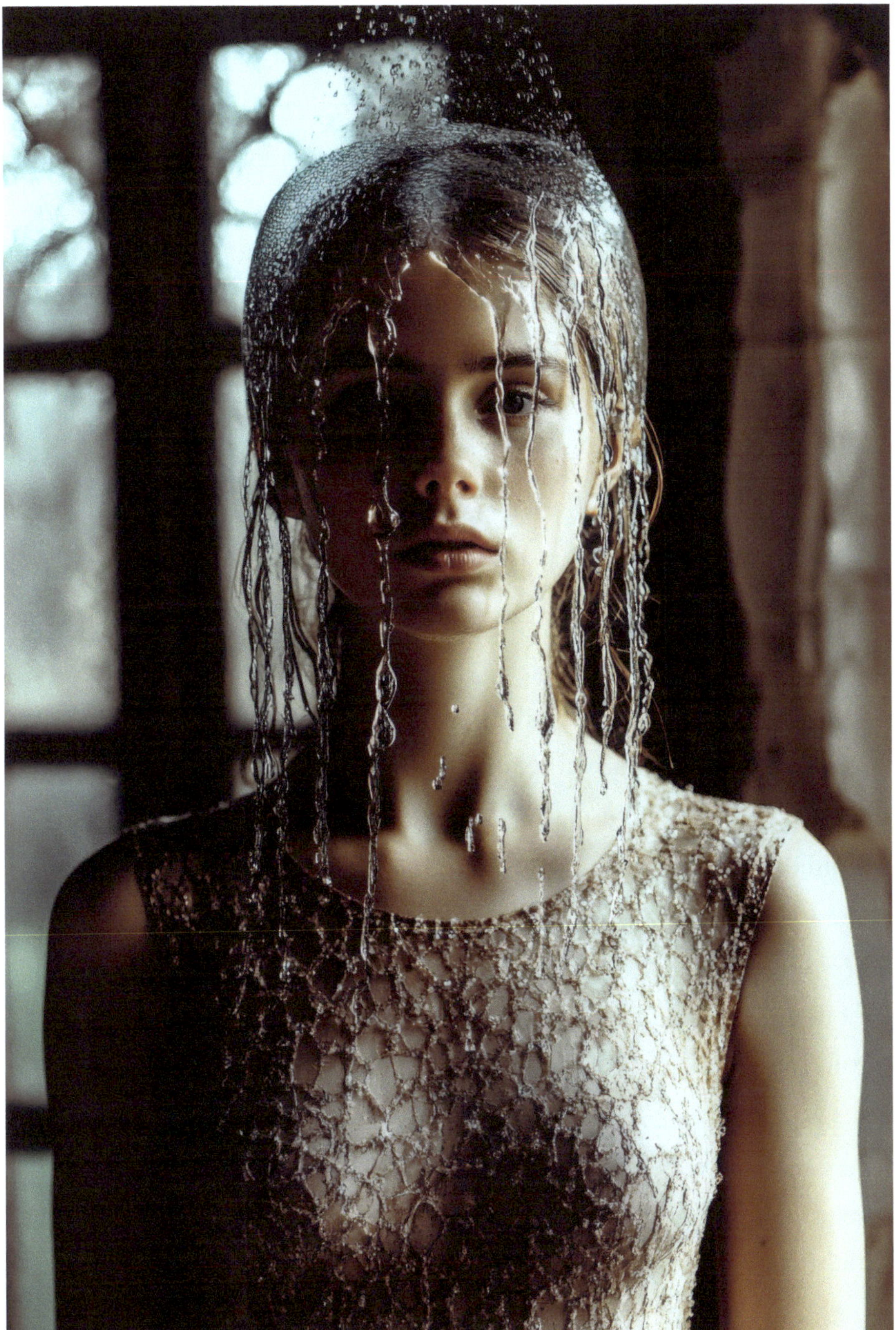

The Collective Unconscious in the Digital Age

The Collective Unconscious in the Digital Age represents the shared psychological landscape and archetypal patterns that emerge and evolve through digital technologies, online communities, and global interconnectivity. In the digital age, the collective unconscious is both amplified and transformed by technology, leading to new forms of shared experiences, symbols, and archetypes that reflect the evolving human psyche in an interconnected world. Key aspects include:

- ***Global Interconnectivity***: The internet and digital platforms facilitate the rapid exchange of ideas, symbols, and narratives across cultural and geographical boundaries, creating a shared global consciousness.
- ***Digital Archetypes***: New archetypal patterns and symbols emerge from the digital age, such as the hacker, the avatar, the troll, the influencer, and the virtual reality explorer.
- ***Virtual Communities***: Online forums, social media platforms, and multiplayer gaming worlds foster collective experiences, shared narratives, and a sense of belonging among dispersed individuals.
- ***Memes and Viral Content***: Memes, trends, and viral content serve as modern folktales or myths, spreading quickly and reflecting the collective thoughts, emotions, and experiences of the digital age.
- ***Artificial Intelligence and Algorithms***: AI and algorithms shape and influence the collective unconscious by curating content, predicting behaviors, and creating personalized digital experiences, raising questions about autonomy, privacy, and the ethical use of technology.

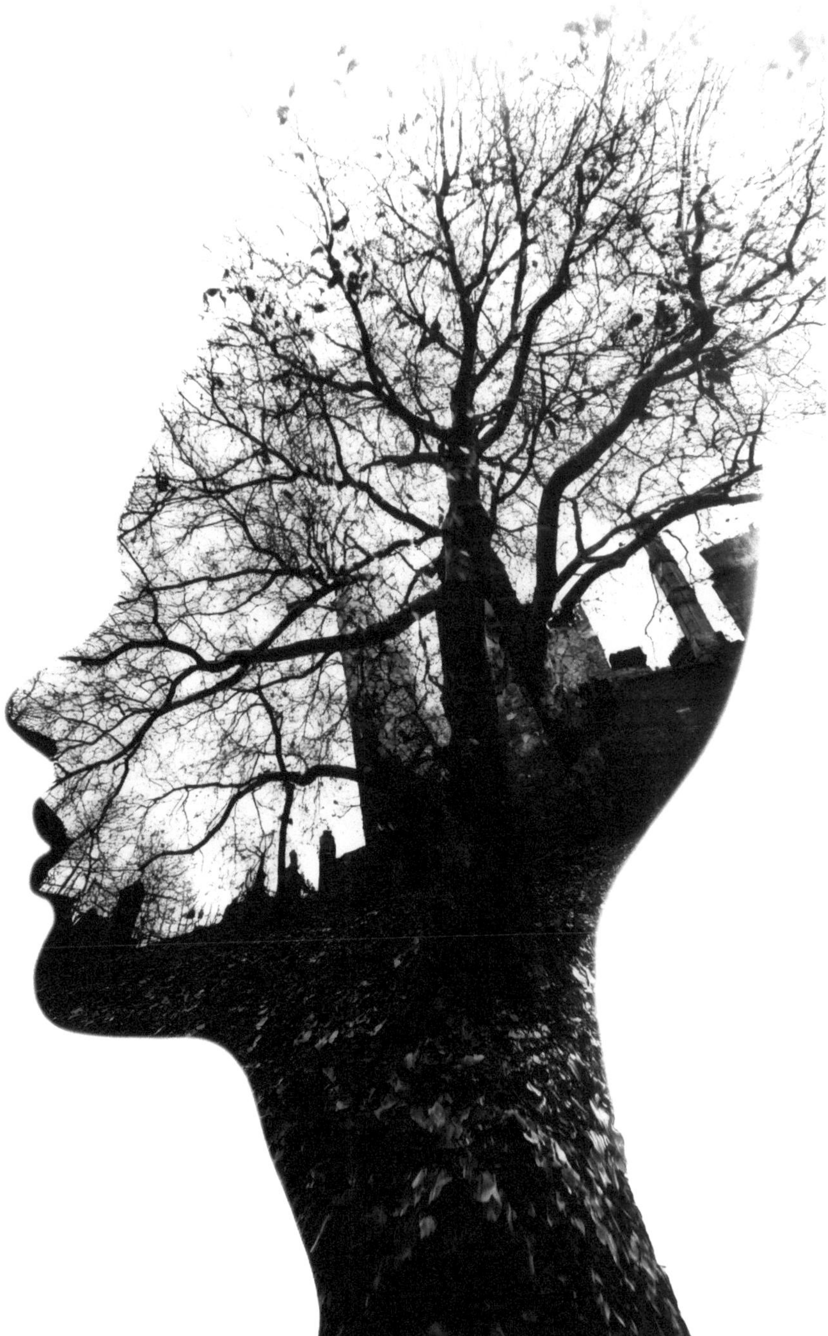

The Contemplative/Reflective Archetype

The **Contemplative/Reflective a**rchetype embodies introspection, thoughtfulness, and a deep inner focus. Individuals or characters aligned with this archetype are often depicted as thoughtful, analytical, and introspective. They tend to prioritize internal reflection over external action, seeking understanding, wisdom, and self-awareness. Key characteristics include:

- ***Introspection***: A strong focus on inner thoughts, feelings, and experiences.
- ***Analysis***: A tendency to examine situations, ideas, and emotions deeply and critically.
- ***Mindfulness***: Being present and aware of one's thoughts, emotions, and surroundings.
- ***Wisdom***: The pursuit of understanding and insight, often through quiet contemplation.

The **Contemplative/Reflective** is often seen in figures like philosophers, scholars, spiritual seekers, and introspective characters in literature and film.

Examples include ***Siddhartha Gautama*** (the Buddha), ***Hamlet*** in Shakespeare's play, and characters who embark on journeys of self-discovery and inner growth.

This archetype highlights the importance of self-reflection, inner wisdom, and the pursuit of deeper understanding.

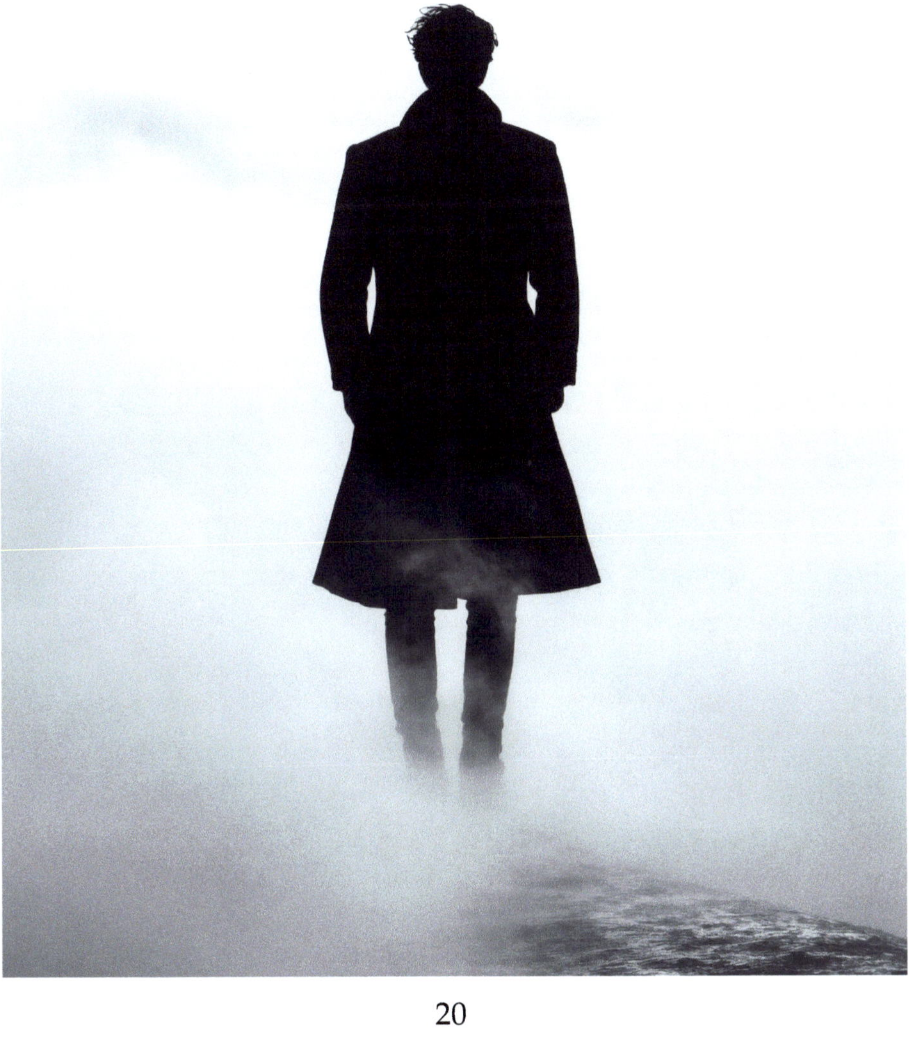

The Creator Archetype

The **Creator** archetype embodies innovation, vision, and the ability to manifest ideas into reality. This archetype represents individuals who are driven to build, design, and bring new things into existence. Key characteristics include:

- ***Visionary***: Possesses a unique perspective and the ability to envision new ideas, projects, or solutions.
- ***Innovative***: Constantly seeks to push boundaries, experiment, and challenge the status quo.
- ***Productive***: Focused on turning ideas into tangible outcomes, whether they are artistic works, inventions, or other creations.
- ***Purposeful***: Often driven by a deeper meaning or goal, aiming to make a lasting impact on the world.
- ***Resourceful***: Adept at problem-solving, adapting, and finding the means to achieve their creative goals.

The **Creator** is often depicted in stories, myths, and cultural narratives as inventors, architects, entrepreneurs, and other innovative individuals who leave a lasting legacy through their creations.

Examples include characters like **Leonardo da Vinci**, **Steve Jobs**, and the inventive, forward-thinking figures portrayed in various narratives.

This archetype highlights the human capacity for innovation, the power of vision, and the drive to bring new ideas to life.

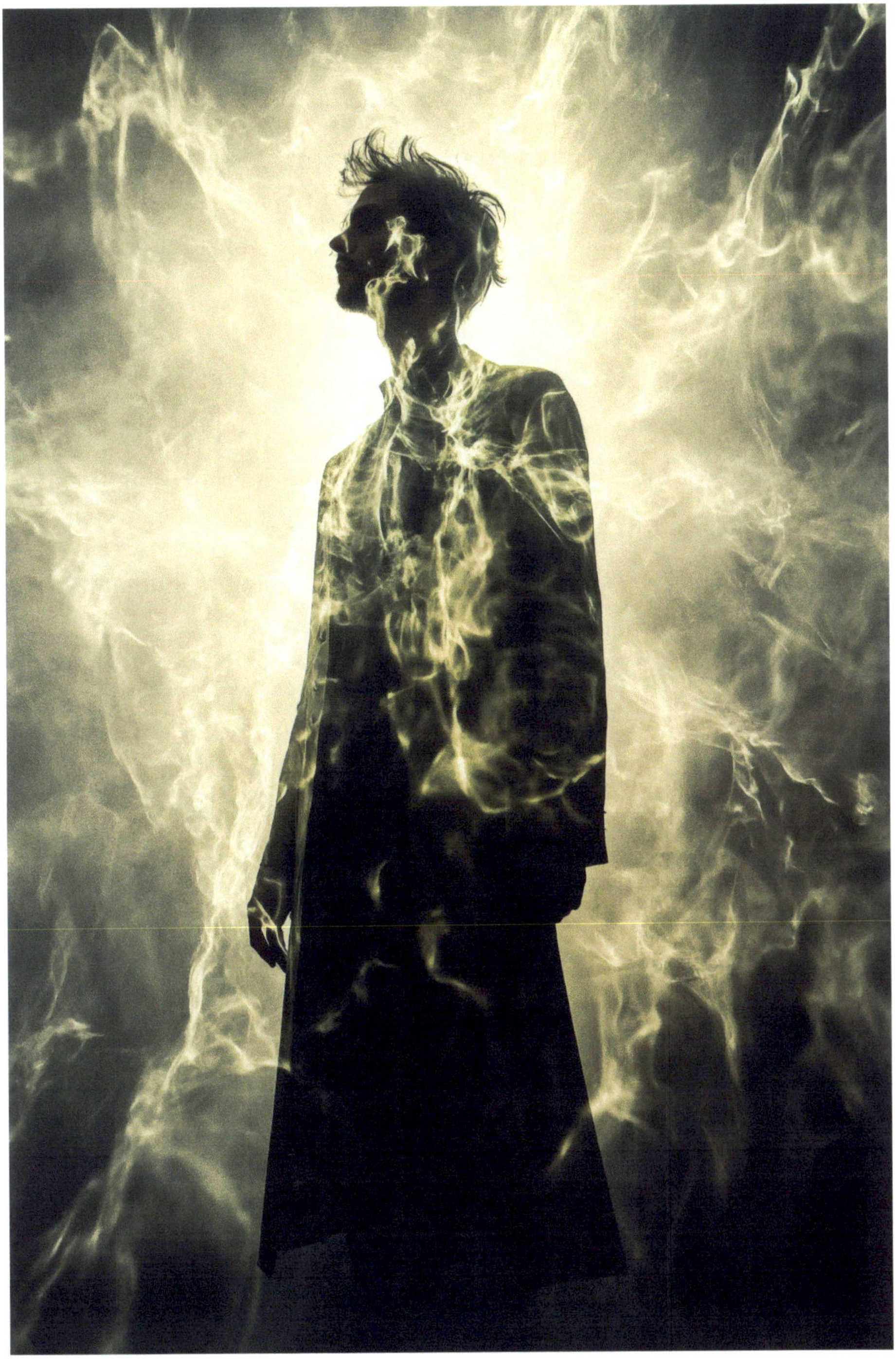

The Cyborg Archetype

The Cyborg Archetype represents the fusion of human and machine, embodying the integration of technology and biology. This archetype explores themes of enhancement, transcendence, and the blurring of boundaries between natural and artificial. Key characteristics include:

- ***Hybrid Nature***: The combination of organic and technological components, creating a being that is part human and part machine.
- ***Enhanced Abilities***: often possesses augmented strength, intelligence, or other capabilities beyond typical human limits.
- ***Identity Crisis***: May struggle with questions of identity, humanity, and the implications of technological integration.
- ***Ethical Dilemmas***: Raises questions about the consequences of over-reliance on technology, the potential loss of humanity, and the ethical considerations of enhancement.

The **Cyborg** is prevalent in science fiction, futuristic narratives, and discussions about the impact of technology on society and human evolution.

Examples include the **Terminator** in the Terminator franchise, the **Borg** in Star Trek, and the **replicants** in Blade Runner.

This archetype highlights the complex interplay between humanity and technology, and challenges traditional notions of humanity and raises questions about identity, consciousness, and what it means to be human.

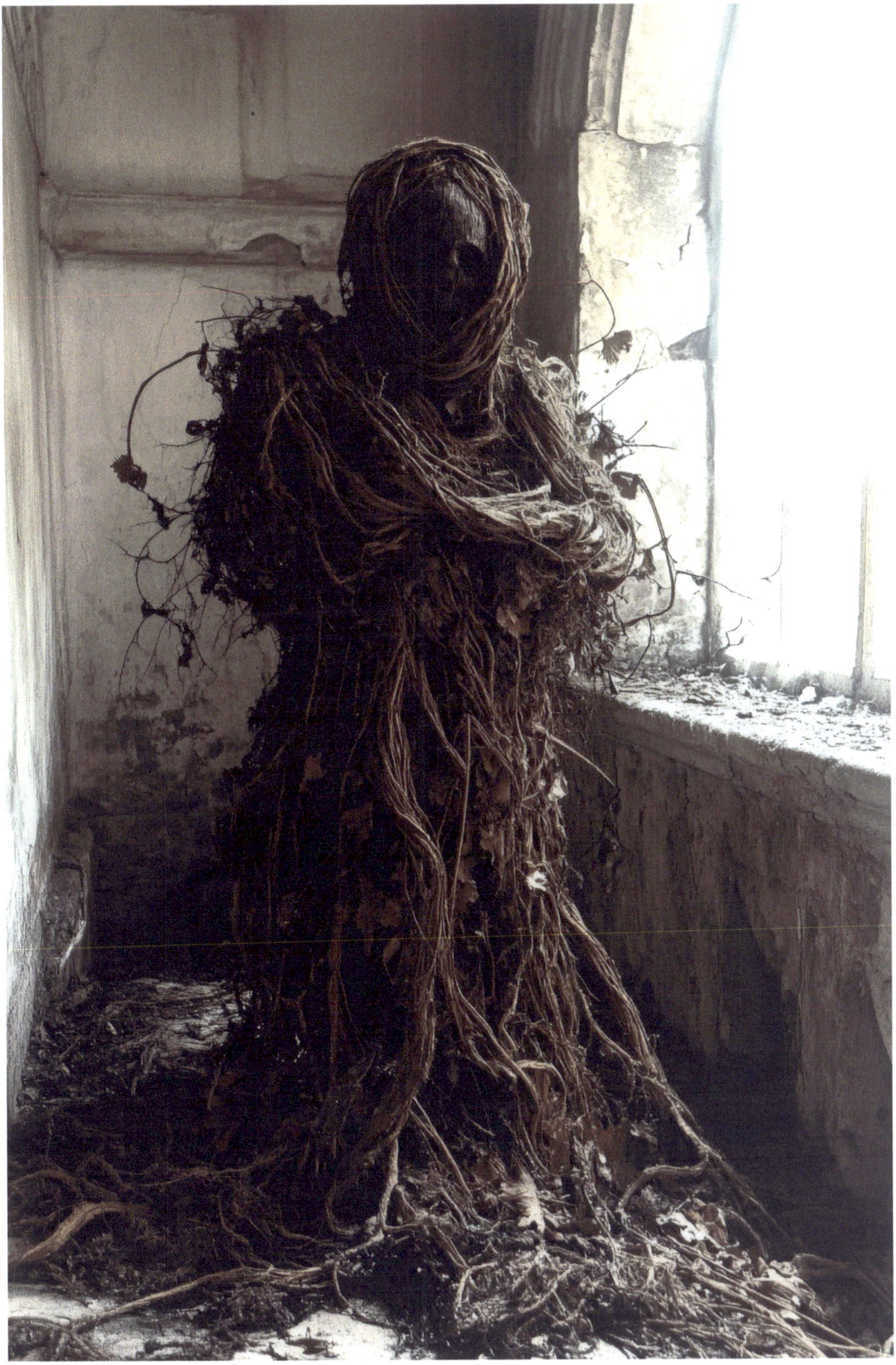

The Divine Child Archetype

The Divine Child Archetype embodies purity, innocence, and the potential for spiritual renewal and redemption. This archetype represents the hope, promise, and transformative power of new beginnings, often symbolizing the salvation or rebirth of a community, culture, or even humanity itself. Key characteristics of the **Divine Child** include:

- ***Innocence***: Radiates purity, vulnerability, and an untainted perspective on the world.
- ***Hope***: Embodies the promise of a brighter future and the potential for positive change.
- ***Renewal***: Brings a sense of rebirth, rejuvenation, or spiritual awakening to those who encounter or believe in them.
- ***Wisdom***: Often possesses an innate understanding of profound truths, offering insights or guidance beyond their years.
- ***Unification***: Has the power to bring people together, healing divisions and fostering a sense of collective purpose or harmony.

The **Divine Child** is often depicted in mythology, religion, and popular culture as characters who bring hope and salvation, symbolize new beginnings and the cycle of life, possess extraordinary gifts or abilities, inspire and unite others, like the protagonists in stories such as **The Golden Compass** or **The Giver**.

This archetype highlights the human longing for hope, renewal, and the transformative power of innocence and new beginnings.

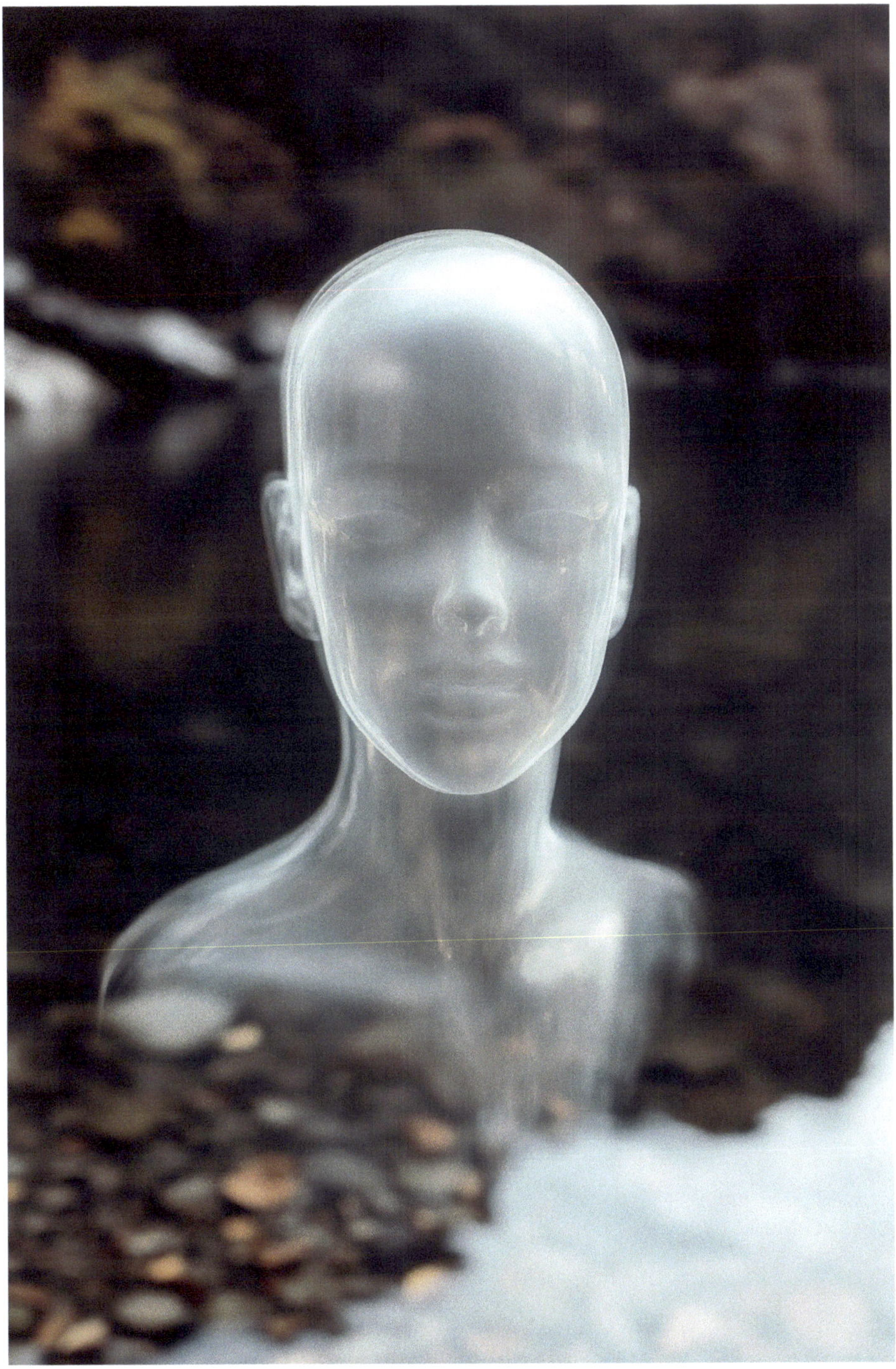

The Dystopian Hero Archetype

The Dystopian Hero Archetype embodies rebellion, resilience, and a struggle against oppressive societies or regimes. This archetype represents individuals who challenge or subvert corrupt, totalitarian, or otherwise flawed systems, often fighting for freedom, justice, or a better world. Key characteristics include:

- ***Defiance***: Stands against oppressive authorities, unjust laws, or societal norms, often at great personal risk.
- ***Courage***: Demonstrates bravery and determination in the face of adversity, willing to make sacrifices for a greater cause.
- ***Critical Thinking***: Questions and challenges the status quo, seeking truth, and exposing the flaws and injustices of the system.
- ***Resourcefulness***: Adaptable and ingenious, finding creative solutions and strategies to outwit or overcome their opponents.
- ***Hope***: Maintains a belief in the possibility of change and a better future, often inspiring others to join their cause.

The **Dystopian Hero** is often depicted in literature, film, and cultural narratives as characters who rebel against oppressive governments or societies, such as: **Winston Smith** (George Orwell's 1984), **Katniss Everdeen** (The Hunger Games), **Neo** (The Matrix), and **Offred** (Margaret Atwood's The Handmaid's Tale).

This archetype highlights the human struggle for freedom, the power of resistance, and the enduring hope for a better world in the face of adversity.

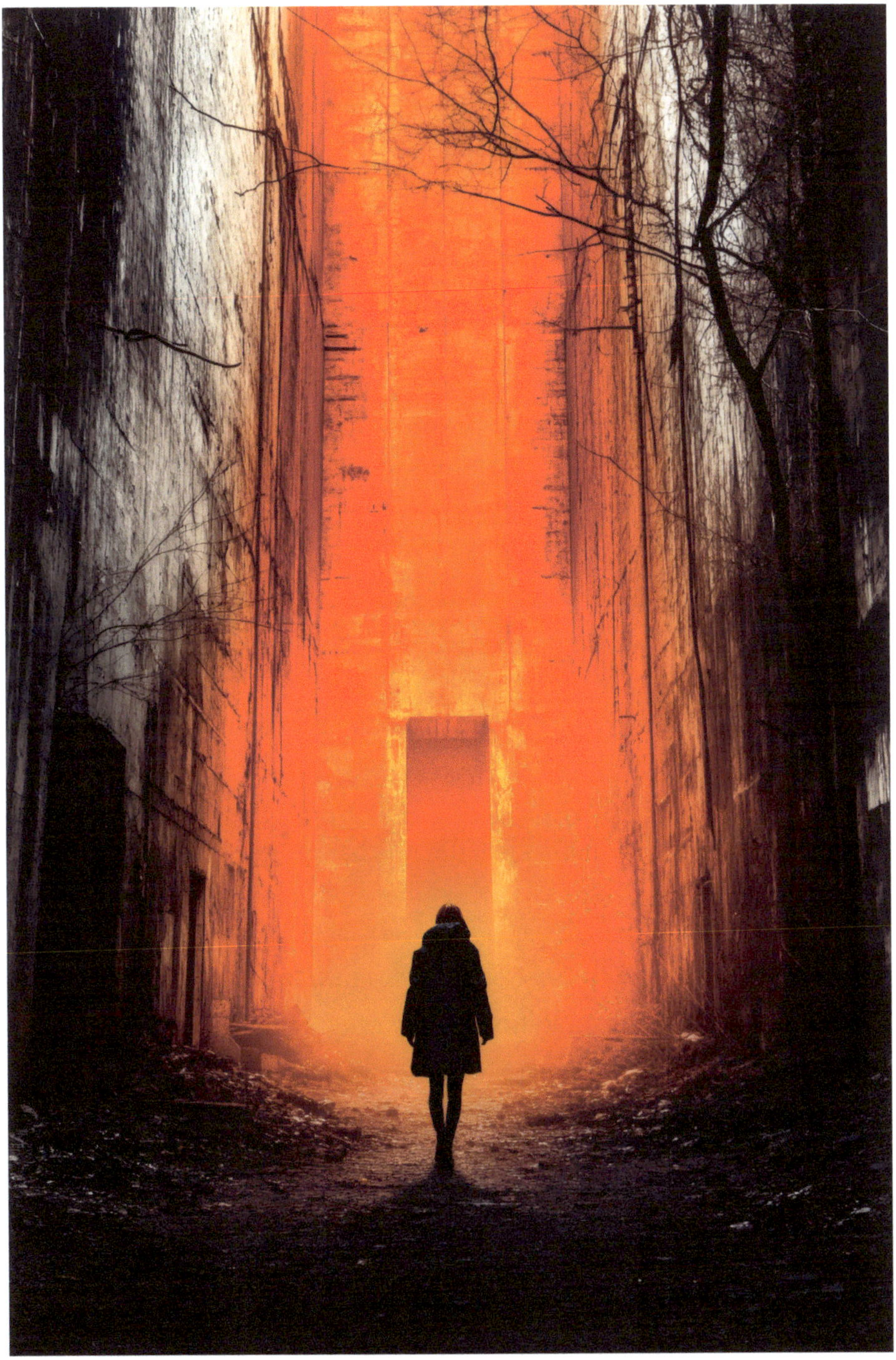

The Elemental Power Archetype

The Elemental Power Archetype represents the fundamental forces of nature, often personified as beings or spirits that embody the essence of earth, air, fire, and water. This archetype symbolizes the raw, primal energies that shape the natural world and influence human experiences. Key characteristics include:

- ***Natural Forces***: Embodies the power of natural elements, such as the strength of earth, the fluidity of water, the heat of fire, and the freedom of air.

- ***Primal Energy***: Represents the untamed, raw power of nature, which can be both creative and destructive.

- ***Connection***: Highlights the interconnectedness of all things and the profound impact of natural forces on human life.

- ***Transformation***: Often associated with change, growth, and the cycles of life, death, and rebirth.

Elemental Powers can be seen in mythologies, folktales, and cultural narratives across various traditions. They often represent creation, destruction, transformation, and the cyclical nature of life. Characters or entities embodying this archetype might possess abilities related to their element, such as control over storms, volcanic activity, plant growth, or ocean currents.

The Elemental Power Archetype highlights the interconnectedness of all things and the profound impact of natural forces on human life.

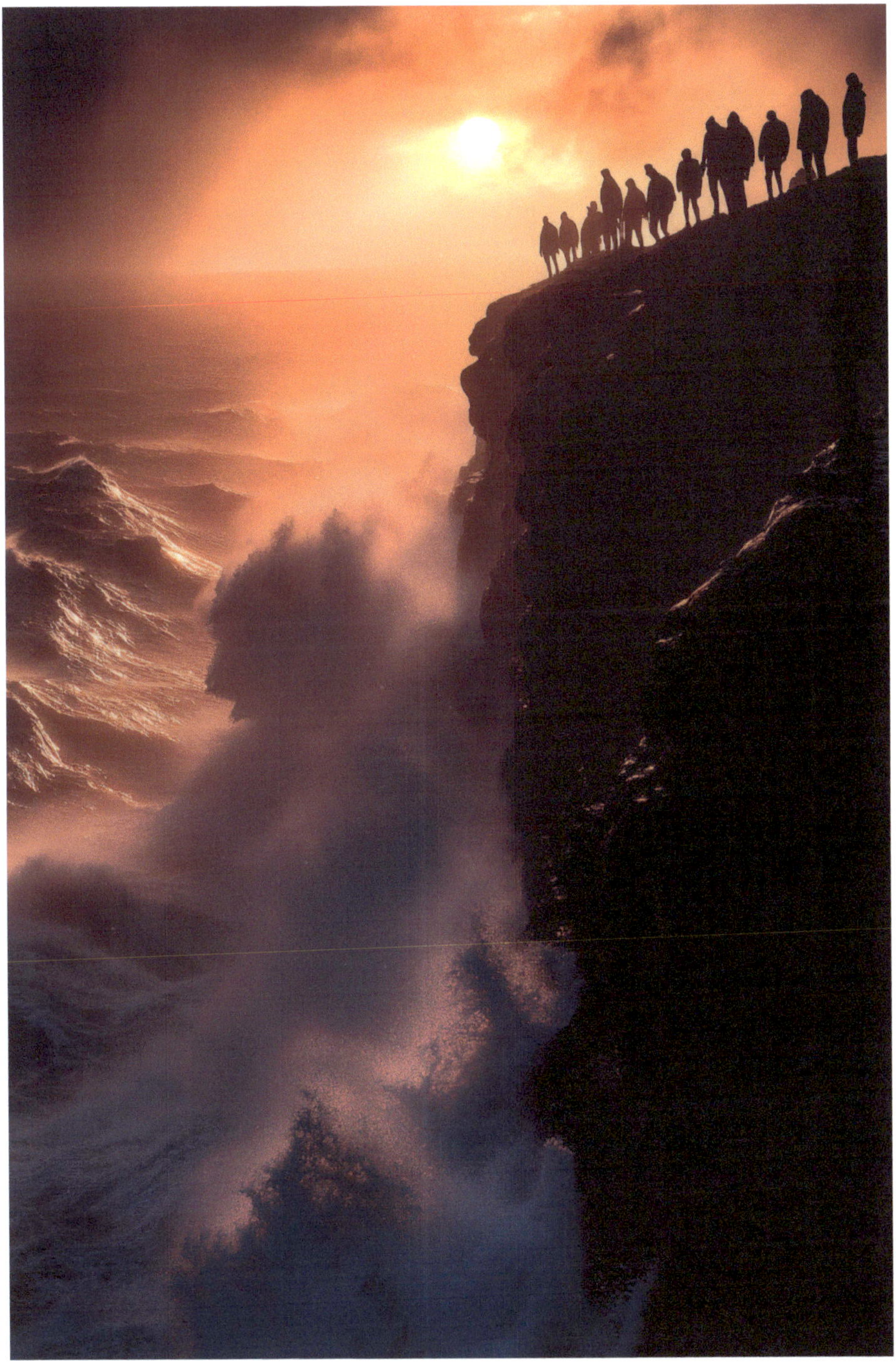

The Endurance of Human Spirit

The Endurance of the Human Spirit Archetype embodies resilience, perseverance, and the indomitable will to overcome adversity. This archetype represents the innate human capacity to endure hardship, maintain hope, and continue striving despite challenging circumstances.

Characters or individuals embodying this archetype often face significant obstacles, such as oppression, hardship, or tragedy, but remain steadfast and determined.

Key aspects of this archetype include:

- ***Resilience***: The ability to bounce back from setbacks and maintain a positive outlook.
- ***Perseverance***: The persistent pursuit of goals despite obstacles or delays.
- ***Hope***: The belief in a better future and the willingness to work towards it.
- ***Courage***: The strength to face and overcome fears or difficulties.

The **Endurance of the Human Spirit** is often depicted in stories of survival, personal growth, and triumph over adversity. It serves as an inspiration and a reminder of the power of the human will.

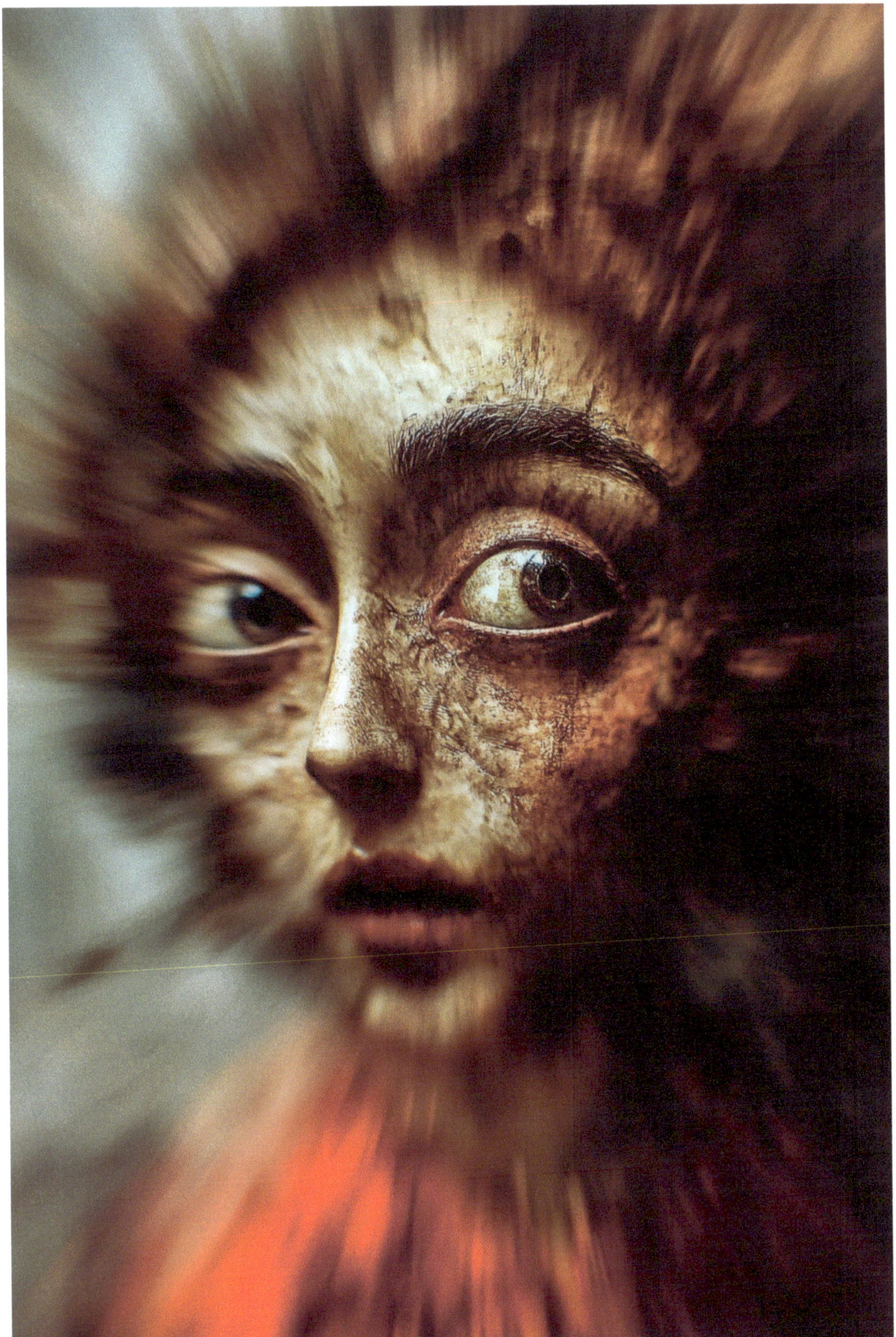

The Everyman Archetype

The Everyman Archetype, also known as the Regular Guy or Gal, represents the average, ordinary person that audiences can easily relate to. This archetype embodies qualities and experiences common to most people, making them approachable and empathetic. Key characteristics of **The Everyman Archetype** include:

- ***Relatability***: They face everyday challenges and have common desires and fears.
- ***Pragmatism***: They pproach situations with practicality and common sense.
- ***Adaptability***: They adjust to various circumstances and make the best of what they have.
- ***Supportive Role***: They serve as a helping hand, loyal friend, or steadfast ally.

The **Everyman** is prevalent in stories, films, and literature, often serving as a bridge between the audience and the narrative, making extraordinary events or themes more accessible and relatable..

Stuart's Commentary

The common human experience includes: We don't know where we come from. We don't know what we really are. We don't know where we are going. We don't know why we are here. We are enigmas to ourselves. We have no choice but to go forward. Or not.

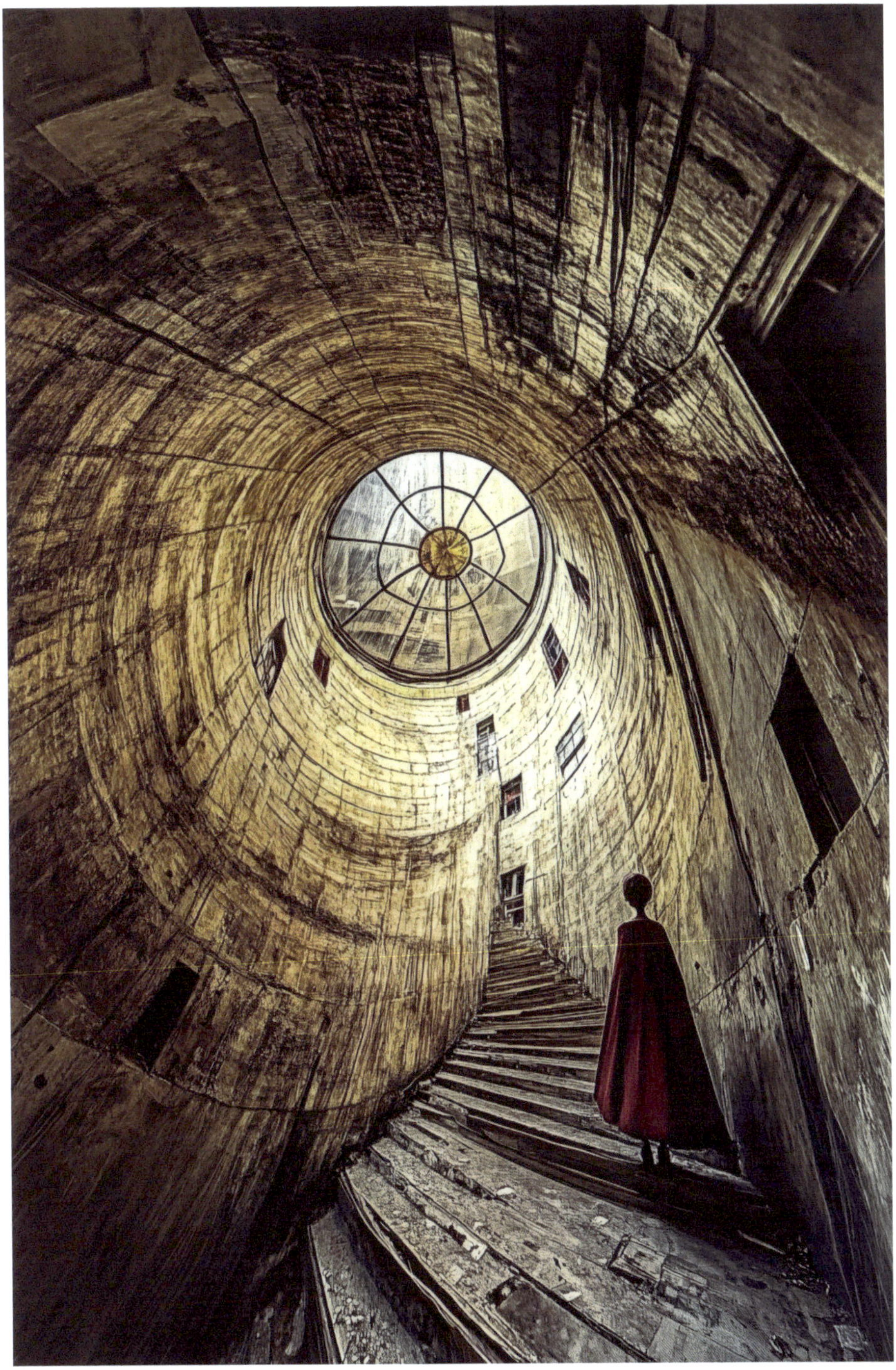

The Explorer/Seafarer Archetype

The Explorer/Seafarer Archetype embodies the spirit of adventure, discovery, and the pursuit of new horizons. This archetype is characterized by a strong desire to venture into the unknown, seek out new experiences, and push beyond established boundaries. Key traits of this archetype include:

- ***Curiosity***: A deep urge to explore and understand the world.
- ***Courage***: The willingness to face risks and challenges in pursuit of discovery.
- ***Independence***: A preference for self-reliance and autonomy.
- ***Restlessness***: A constant drive to move forward and avoid stagnation.

The **Explorer/Seafarer** is often depicted in stories of journeying, quests, and adventures. They can be seen in characters who set sail on voyages, traverse uncharted territories, or embark on personal journeys of self-discovery.

This archetype represents the human impulse to expand our knowledge, challenge our limits, and find our place in the world.

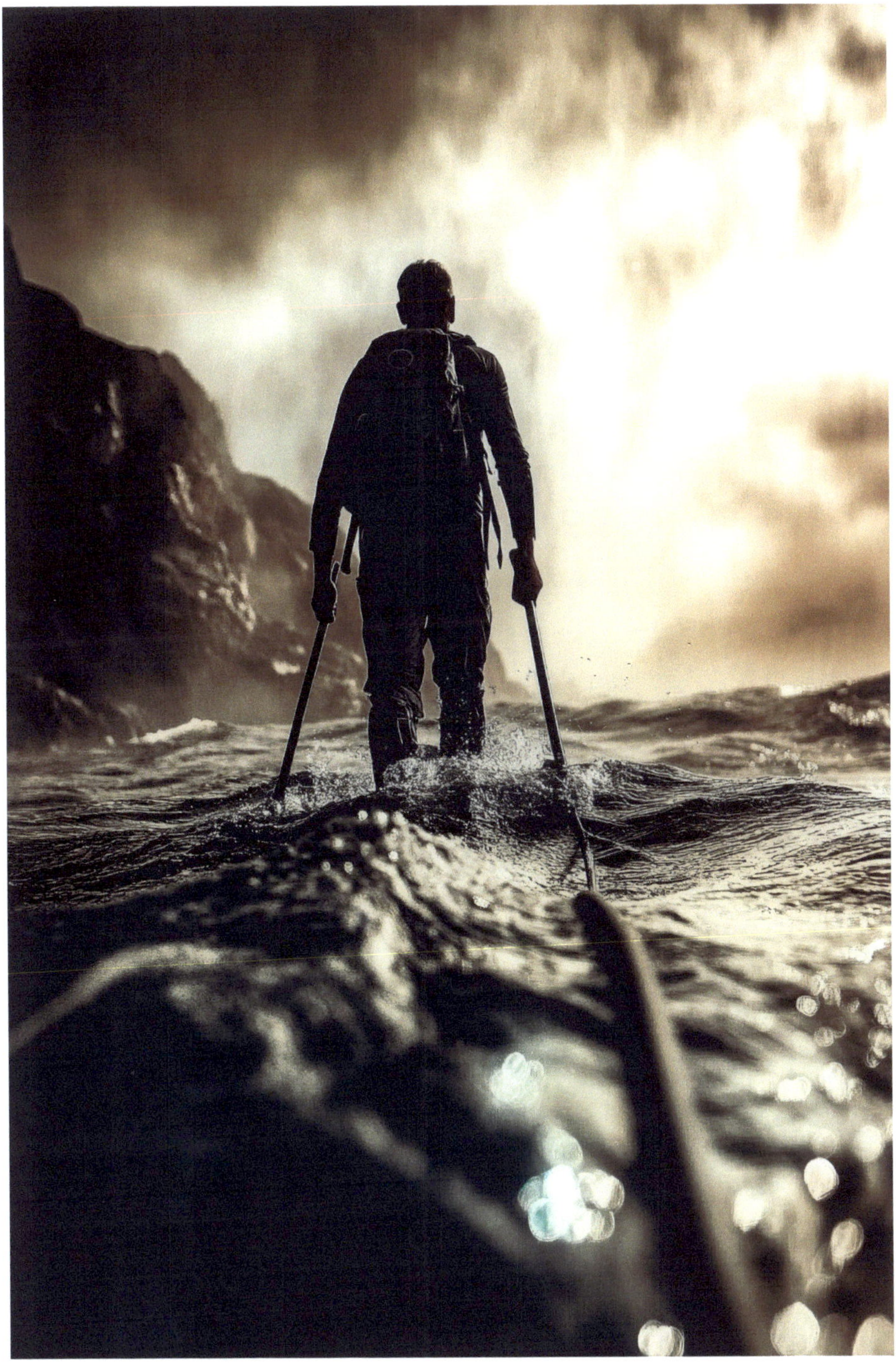

The Explorer/Seeker Archetype

The Explorer/Seeker Archetype embodies curiosity, adventure, and a deep-seated desire to discover new horizons, experiences, or truths. This archetype represents individuals who are driven to venture into the unknown, challenge their limits, and expand their understanding of the world and themselves. Key characteristics include:

- ***Curiosity***: A strong desire to learn, investigate, and uncover hidden knowledge or mysteries.
- ***Adventurousness***: A willingness to take risks, embrace challenges, and step outside of their comfort zone.
- ***Independence***: often values autonomy, self-reliance, and the freedom to forge their own path.
- ***Restlessness***: May be constantly driven to seek out new experiences, experiences, or challenges, making it difficult for them to settle down or remain content with the status quo.
- ***Growth***: Sees personal evolution, self-discovery, and transformation as essential aspects of their journey.

The **Explorer/Seeker** is often depicted in literature, film, and popular culture as characters who embark on epic quests or journeys, pursue spiritual or philosophical truths, explore new frontiers and cultures, or seek personal growth and transformation.

This archetype highlights the human desire for adventure, the power of curiosity, and the potential for personal growth and self-discovery through the exploration of the unknown.

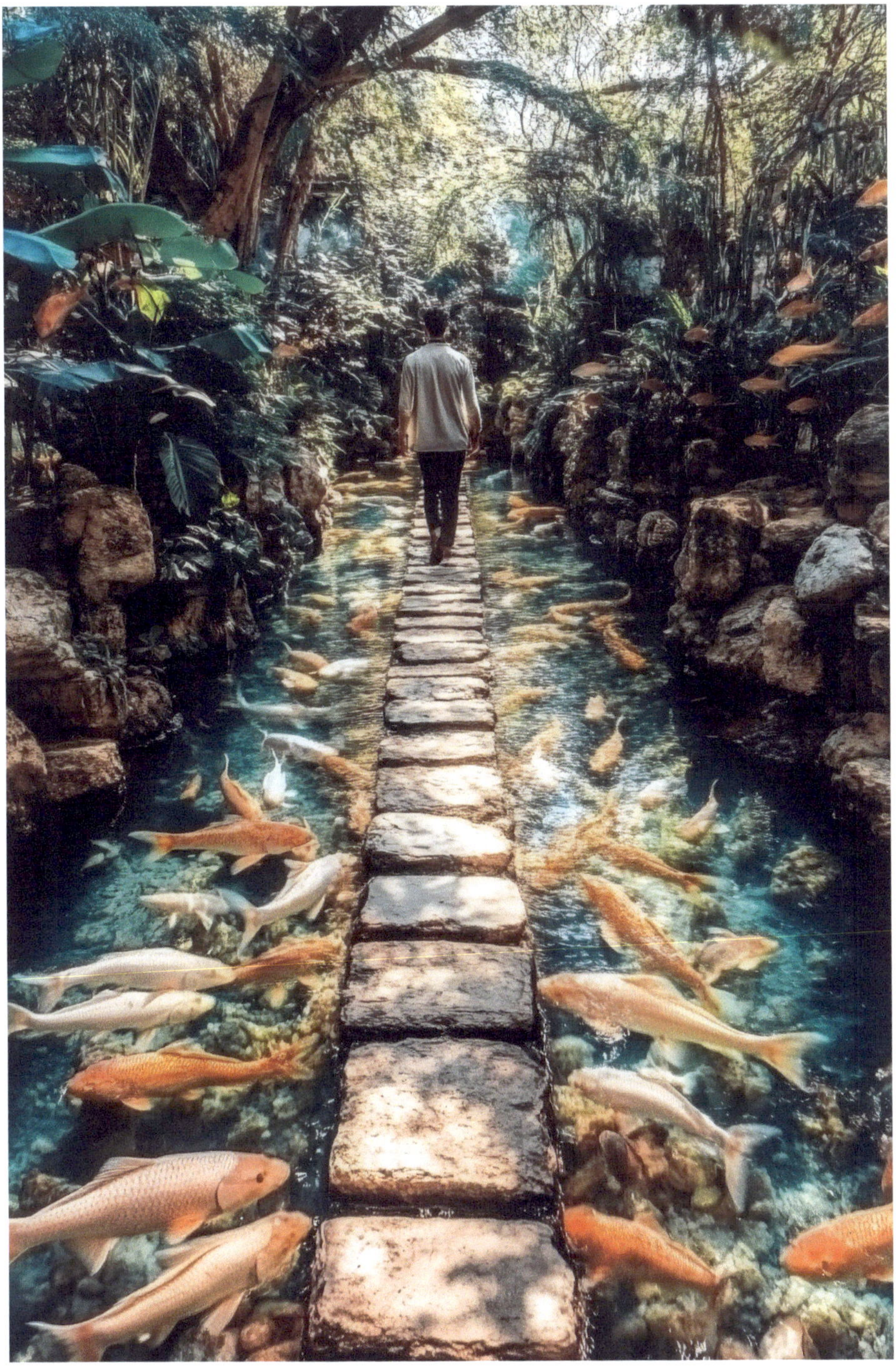

The Feminine Archetype

The Feminine Archetype embodies qualities and characteristics traditionally associated with women and the feminine principle. This archetype is often characterized by:

- ***Nurturing***: A tendency to care for, support, and protect others.
- ***Intuition***: A strong connection to inner wisdom and emotions.
- ***Creativity***: An ability to bring forth new ideas, projects, or life.
- ***Receptivity***: Openness to receiving, adapting, and embracing change.
- ***Interconnectedness***: A focus on relationships, community, and the web of life.

The Feminine Archetype is often depicted in myths, stories, and cultural symbols as mothers, goddesses, healers, and creatives. It represents the life-giving, nurturing, and intuitive aspects of human nature, fostering growth, connection, and emotional depth.

Examples of the **Feminine** can be found across various cultures and historical periods, reflecting the universal significance of feminine qualities in the human experience.

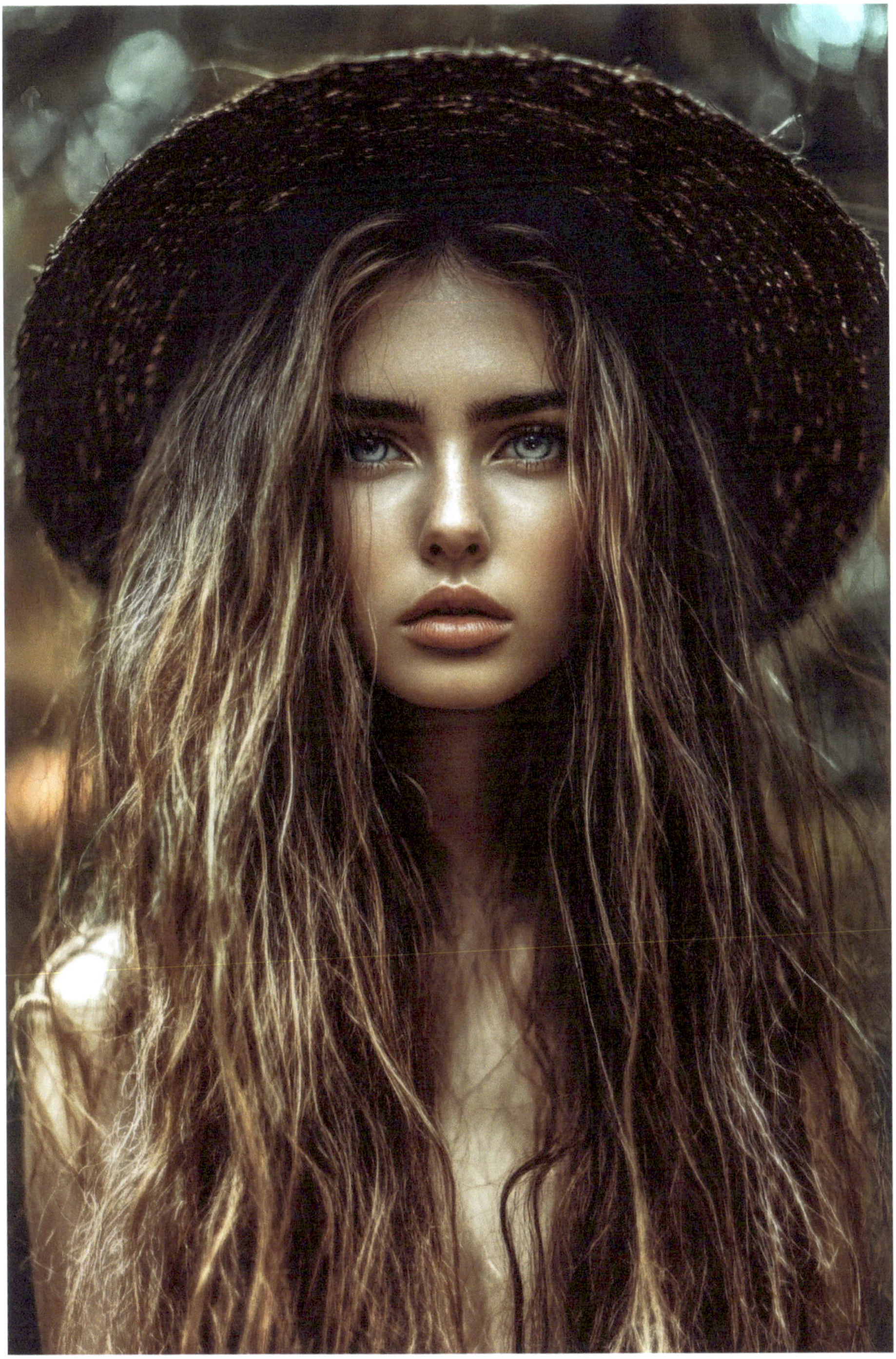

The Fragmented Self Archetype

The Fragmented Self Archetype represents a state of inner division, conflict, or disintegration within an individual's psyche. This archetype embodies the struggle between different aspects of the self, often resulting in feelings of confusion, turmoil, and a lack of cohesive identity. Key characteristics include:

- ***Inner Conflict***: A battle between competing desires, beliefs, or emotions.
- ***Identity Crisis***: A sense of uncertainty or confusion about one's true self or purpose.
- ***Duality***: The presence of opposing forces or personas within the individual.
- ***Disconnection***: A feeling of detachment from one's emotions, thoughts, or experiences.

The **Fragmented Self** is often depicted in stories of internal struggle, psychological turmoil, and the search for self-understanding. It can be seen in characters who grapple with multiple personalities, alter egos, or profound existential questions.

This archetype highlights the human experience of feeling divided or lost, and the journey towards integration, wholeness, and self-acceptance.

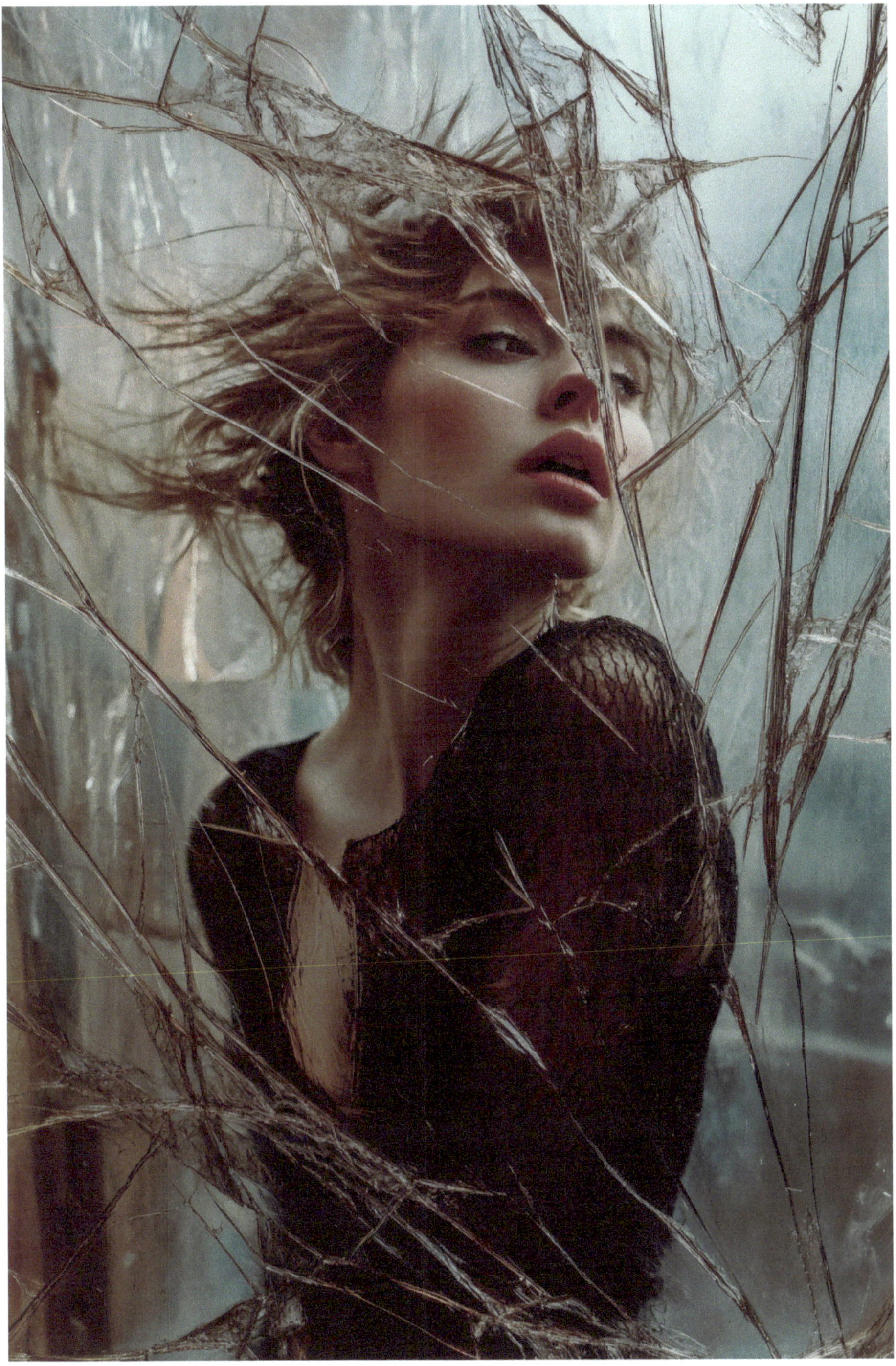

The Hermit Archetype

The Hermit Archetype embodies solitude, introspection, and the search for inner wisdom and enlightenment. This archetype represents individuals who withdraw from society to seek understanding, spiritual growth, or personal insight. Key characteristics include:

- ***Solitude***: Chooses to live in isolation or seclusion, away from the distractions and influences of the world.
- ***Introspection***: Focuses on inner reflection, self-examination, and the exploration of their thoughts, emotions, and spirituality.
- ***Wisdom***: Often seeks or possesses deep understanding, knowledge, or spiritual awareness, which may be shared with others who venture into their domain.
- ***Asceticism***: May adopt a simple, minimalist lifestyle, renouncing material possessions, comforts, or worldly desires in pursuit of spiritual goals.
- ***Guidance***: Can serve as a mentor, advisor, or spiritual guide to those who seek their counsel, offering insights gained from their solitary contemplation.

The **Hermit** is often depicted in literature, film, and popular culture as: religious or spiritual figures; wise, reclusive characters who offer guidance to heroes or seekers; individuals who withdraw from society to grapple with personal demons or past traumas, and mysterious; solitary figures who inhabit remote or hidden locations. This archetype highlights the potential for spiritual growth and wisdom through withdrawal from the world and exploration of the inner self.

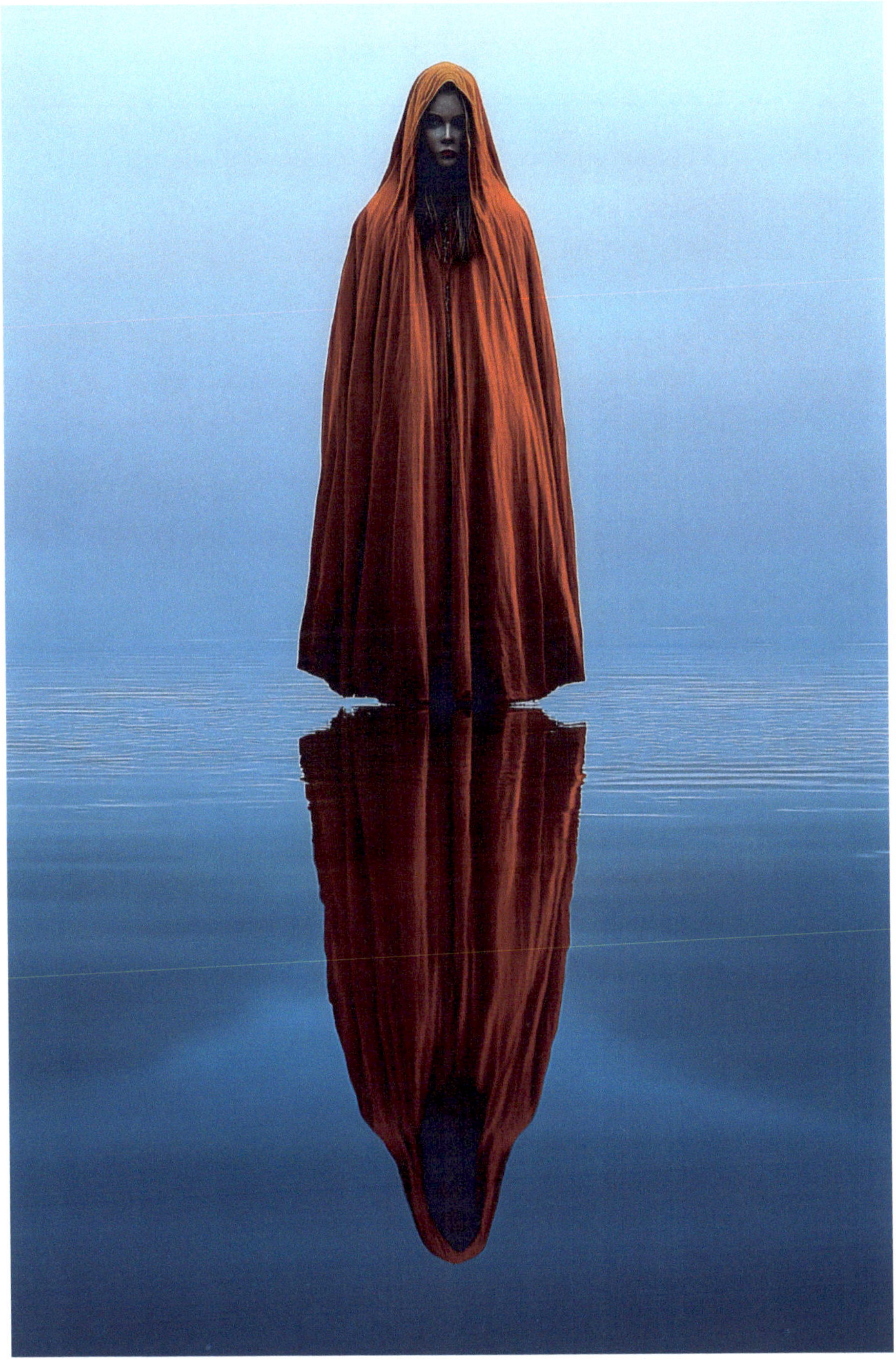

The Hero Archetypes

The Hero Archetypes embody the diverse journeys, challenges, and triumphs of protagonists who face adversity, grow, and ultimately achieve their goals. Key hero archetypes include:

- ***The Classic Hero*** embarks on a quest or adventure to save the day, defeat evil, or achieve a noble goal. He possesses courage, strength, and determination, often facing and overcoming formidable obstacles.
- ***The Anti-Hero*** possesses flawed or morally ambiguous characteristics, often operating outside conventional norms or expectations. He may have a complex past, questionable motives, or a disregard for rules and authority.
- ***The Reluctant Hero*** initially avoids or resists the call to adventure, but ultimately steps up to face the challenge. He may be thrust into the hero's role by circumstance, duty, or the need to protect others.
- ***The Tragic Hero*** possesses a fatal flaw or makes a critical error in judgment, leading to their downfall or demise. He often faces insurmountable odds, impossible choices, or the consequences of their own actions.
- **The Everyday Hero** faces and overcomes the challenges of ordinary life, demonstrating resilience, determination, and personal growth. He may not possess extraordinary abilities or face epic battles.
- ***The Byronic Hero*** is a charismatic, passionate, and flawed figure who often defies conventions and embodies a dark, brooding intensity. He may be driven by a complex past, unrequited love, or a desire for revenge.

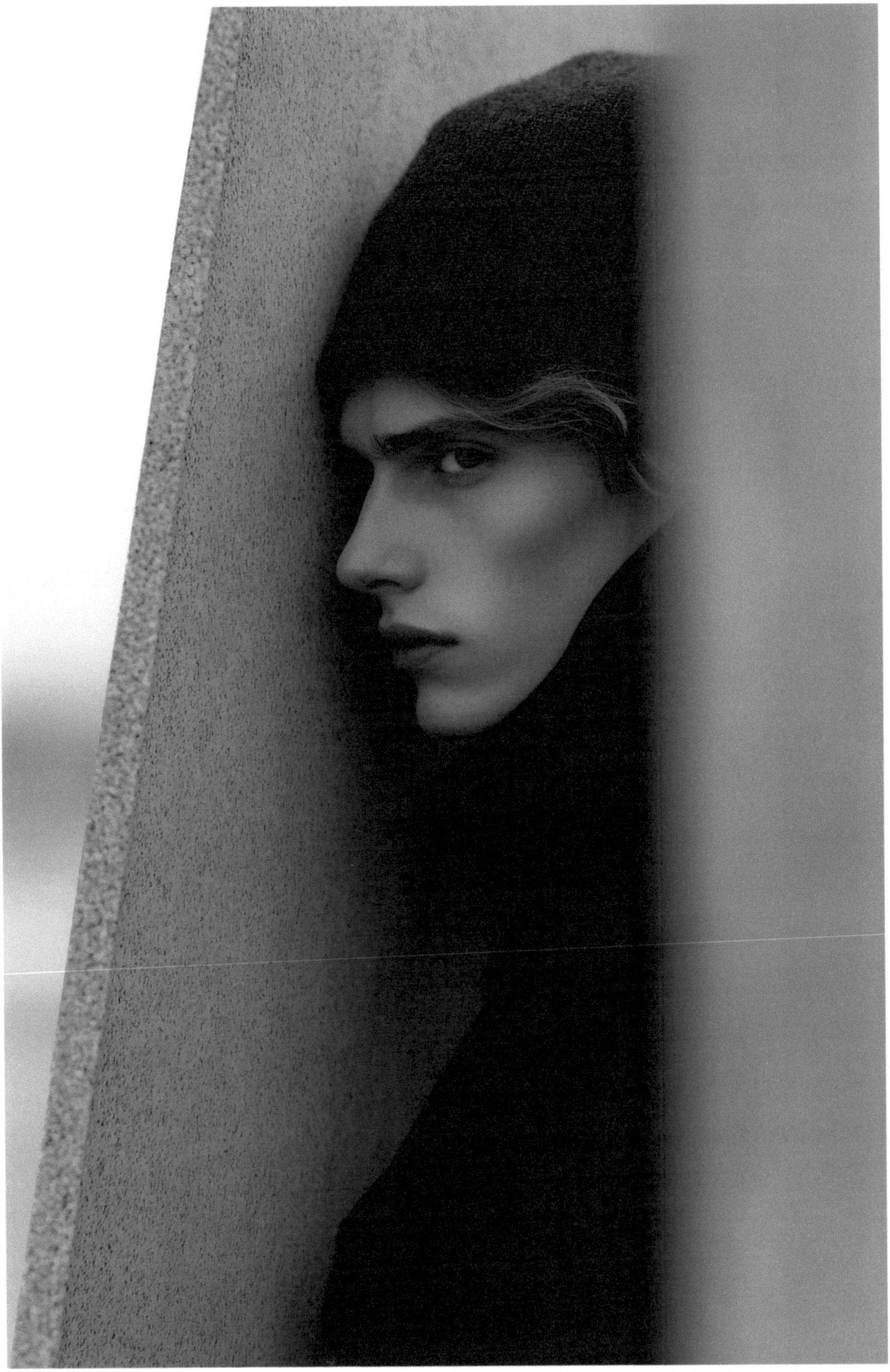

The Heroine Archetypes

The Heroine Archetypes embody the diverse strengths, journeys, and experiences of female protagonists, challenging traditional gender roles and highlighting the multifaceted nature of feminine power and resilience. Key heroine archetypes include:

- ***The Warrior Heroine*** embodies physical strength, courage, and combat skills. She fights for justice, protects others, and challenges oppression.
- ***The Magical/Mystical Heroine*** possesses supernatural abilities, intuition, or spiritual wisdom. She explores and manipulates the forces of nature, the divine, or the unknown.
- ***The Journeying Heroine*** embarks on a quest or adventure, seeking personal growth, truth, or enlightenment. She encounters challenges, learns lessons, and discovers her true self along the way.
- ***The Enduring Heroine*** faces adversity, hardship, or oppression with resilience, determination, and unyielding spirit. She survives and perseveres, often inspiring others with her strength and endurance.
- ***The Nurturing Heroine*** demonstrates empathy, compassion, and the ability to care for and support others. She heals, guides, and inspires those around her, often serving as a mentor, teacher, or caregiver.
- ***The Rebellious Heroine*** defies conventions, challenges authority, and fights for freedom and independence.She breaks the mold, forges her own path, and inspires others to question the status quo.

These heroine archetypes showcase the multifaceted nature of feminine power, resilience, and growth.

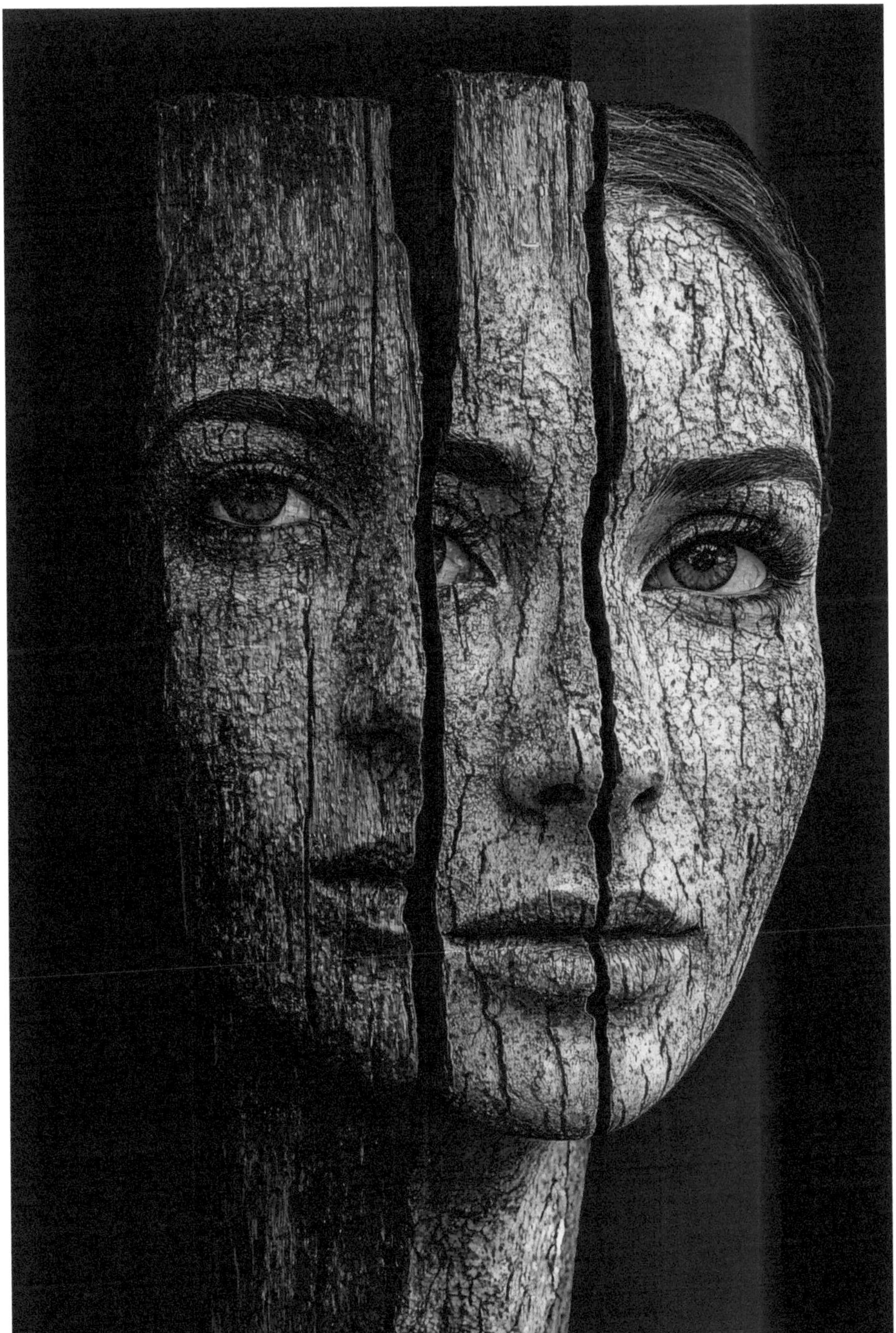

The Hero's Journey

The Hero's Journey is a common storytelling archetype that outlines the path of a hero who ventures out, faces challenges, and ultimately transforms or triumphs. This archetype, popularized by mythologist Joseph Campbell, follows a structured narrative pattern with key stages:

The Hero's Journey starts with ***The Call to Adventure***, which is initially refused, and moves on to reach a climactic ***Ordeal***, from which the hero gains a ***Reward***, and must then take ***The Road Back*** to ***Return with the Elixir***, but along the way confronts ***Resurrection*** when the hero faces a final, transformative challenge that leads to rebirth or renewal. The hero returns to their ordinary world, bringing back the knowledge, reward, or change they have gained to benefit others.

The Hero's Journey archetype is prevalent in myths, stories, and films across cultures, reflecting the universal human experience of growth, transformation, and overcoming adversity.

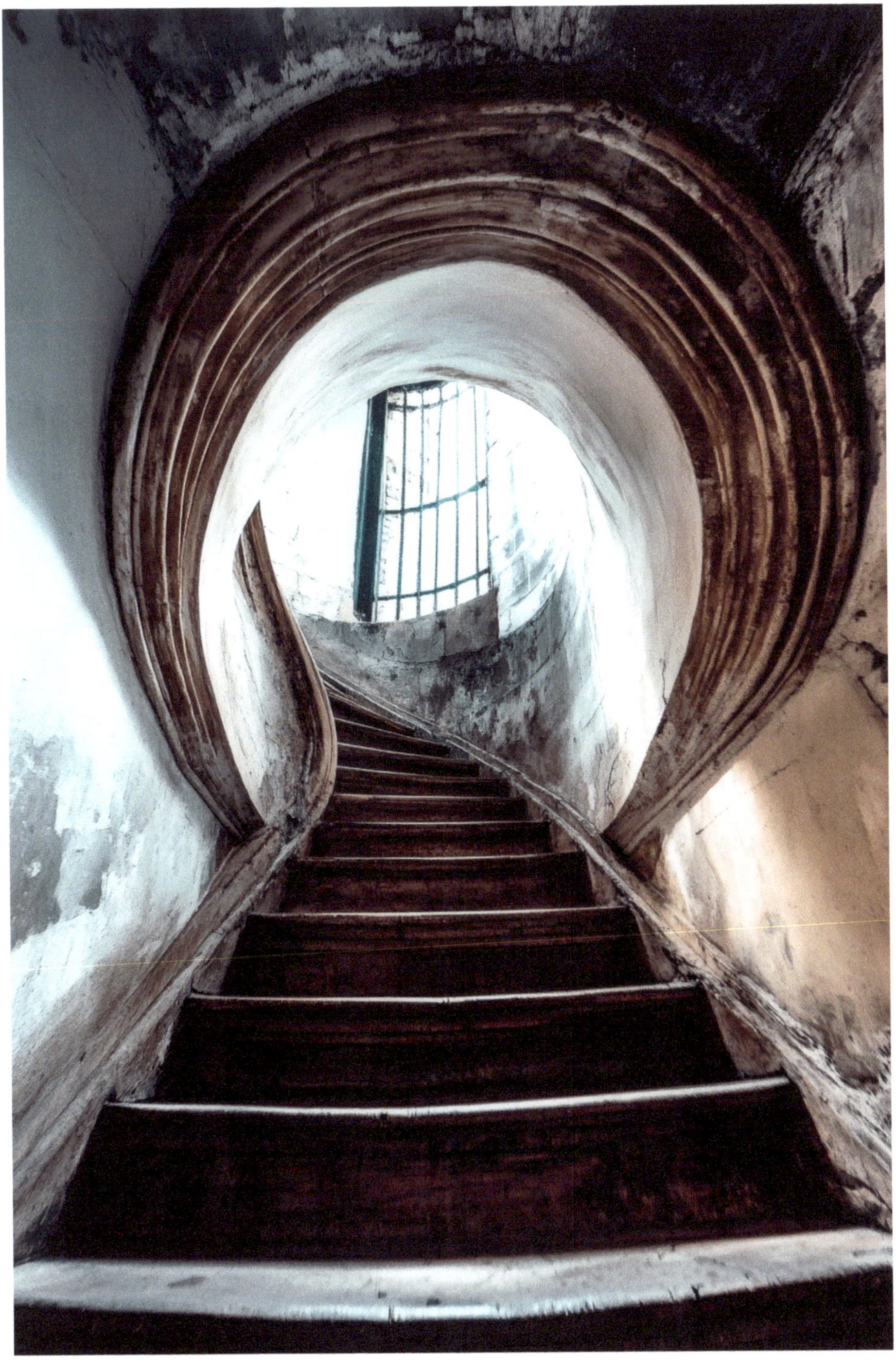

The Hero/Villain Duality

The Hero/Villain Duality archetype explores the interconnectedness and often blurred line between good and evil within a single character or narrative. This archetype highlights the complex nature of morality and the potential for heroes to possess dark qualities or for villains to exhibit redeeming traits. Key aspects include:

- ***Moral Ambiguity***: Characters exhibit a mix of noble and malicious intentions or actions.
- ***Transformation***: Characters may shift between heroic and villainous roles based on their choices and circumstances.
- ***Inner Conflict***: Characters grapple with opposing forces or impulses within themselves.
- ***Redemption or Fall***: Characters may seek redemption for past wrongs or face a tragic fall from grace.

This **Hero/Villain** is often depicted in stories featuring anti-heroes, complex villains, or characters who struggle with their darker impulses. It emphasizes the human capacity for both good and evil, and the complex nature of moral decision-making.

Examples can be found in various narratives, such as Victor Hugo's ***Les Misérables***, the character of ***Darth Vader*** in Star Wars, and numerous other stories that explore the grey areas of morality.

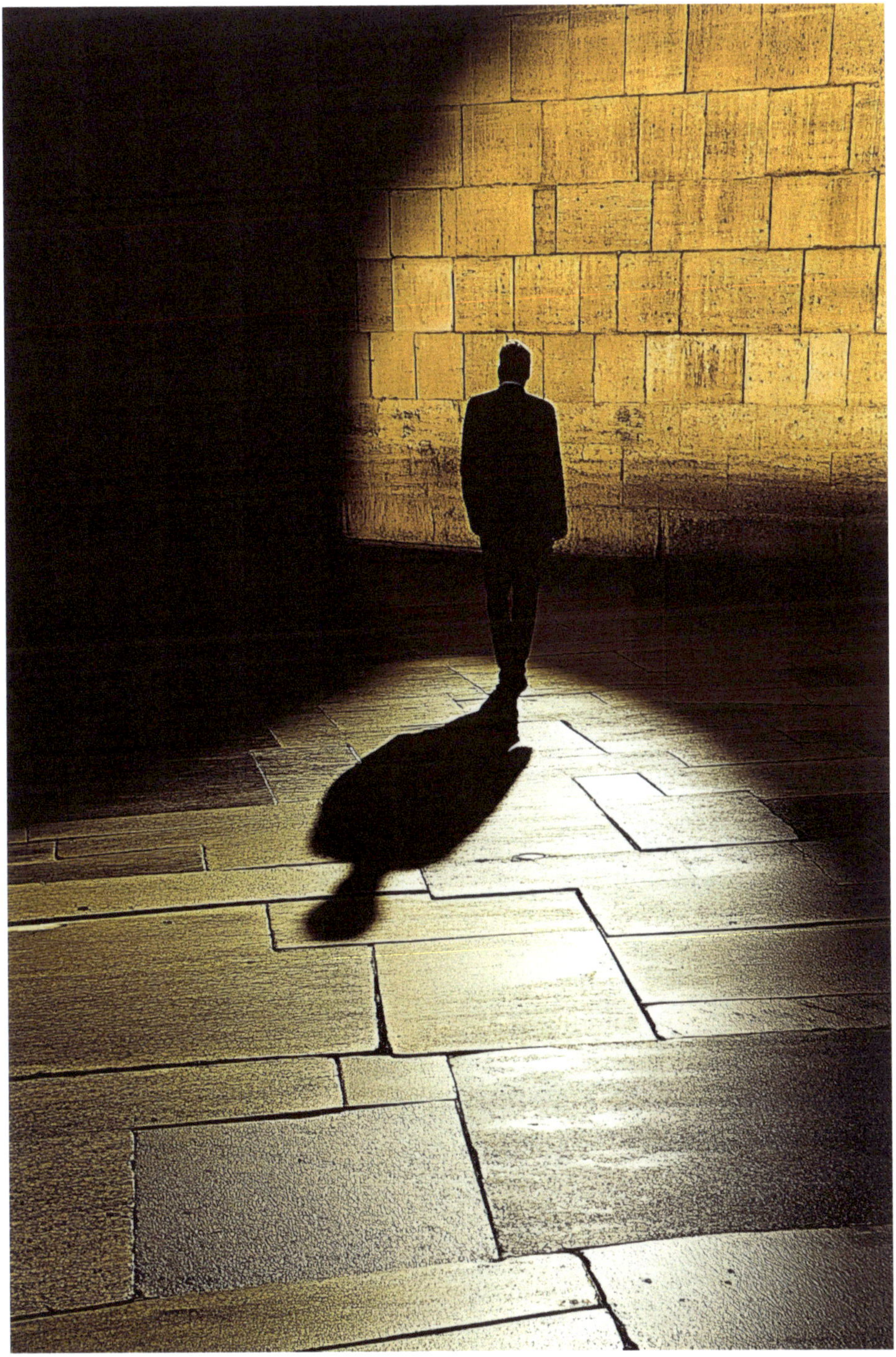

The Innocent Archetype

The Innocent Archetype embodies purity, simplicity, and a sense of wonder or naivety in perceiving the world. This archetype represents individuals who are untainted by the complexities and cynicism of life, often seeing the good in others and maintaining a hopeful, optimistic outlook. Key characteristics include:

- ***Purity***: Uncorrupted and unsullied by negative experiences or influences.
- ***Trusting***: Possesses a strong faith in the inherent goodness of people and the world.
- ***Optimistic***: Maintains a hopeful, positive outlook, even in the face of adversity.
- ***Simplicity***: Appreciates the simple pleasures and beauties of life, often finding joy in everyday experiences.
- ***Naivety***: May be inexperienced or sheltered, leading to a lack of worldly wisdom or understanding of complex situations.

The **Innocent** is often depicted in literature, film, and cultural narratives as children, idealistic young adults, or characters who maintain a sense of wonder and purity despite the challenges they face. Examples include characters like **Dorothy Gale** from The Wizard of Oz, **Forrest Gump** from the eponymous film, and other figures who embody the qualities of innocence, hope, and simplicity.

This archetype highlights the human capacity for faith, optimism, and the appreciation of life's simple joys.

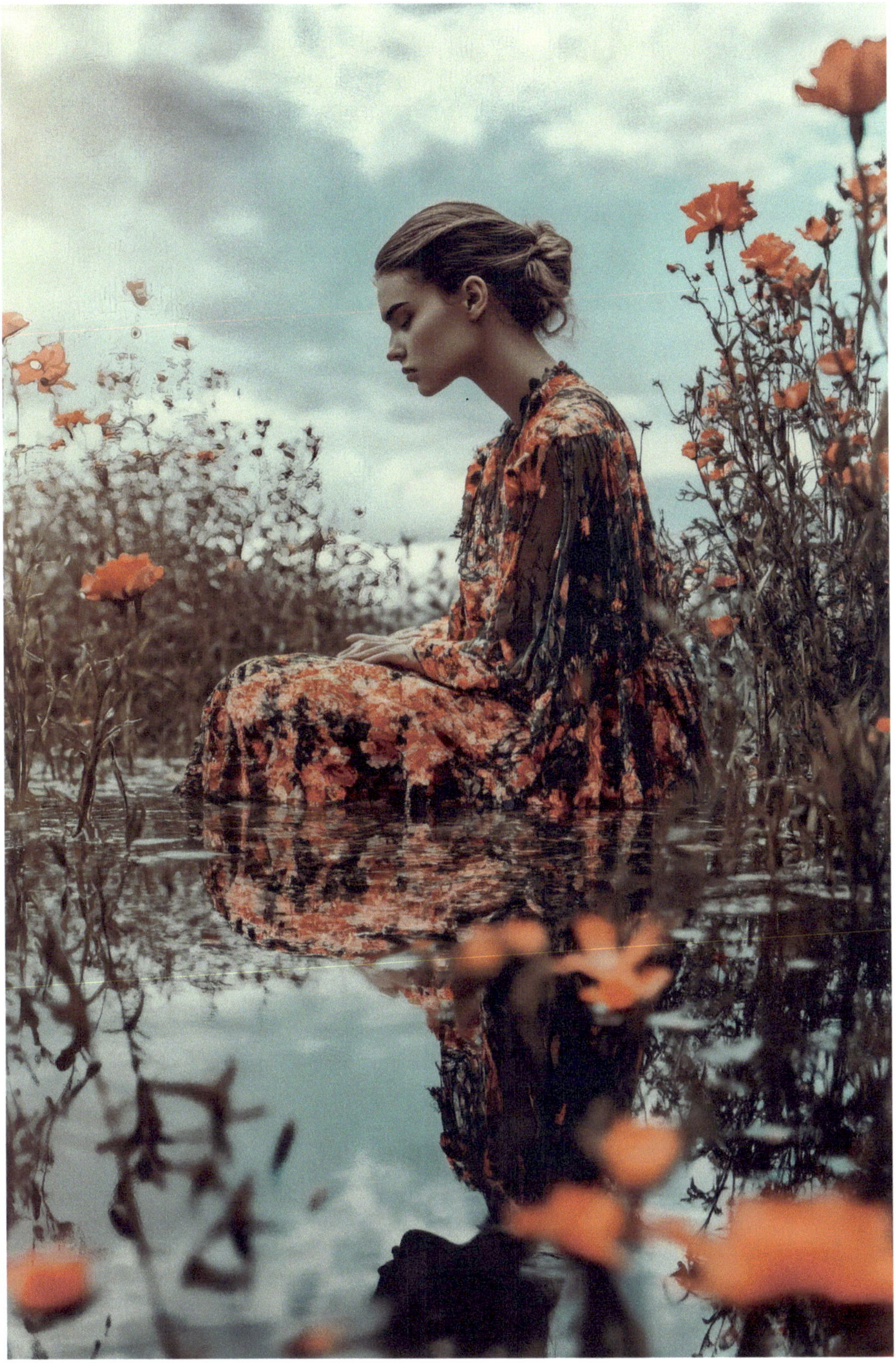

The Inventor Archetype

The Inventor Archetype embodies innovation, problem-solving, and the ability to create practical solutions and new technologies. This archetype represents individuals who are driven by a desire to build, design, and improve the world around them through their ingenious ideas and creations. Key characteristics include:

- ***Creativity***: Possesses a strong imagination and the ability to envision and develop new ideas, devices, or systems.
- ***Problem-Solving***: Excels at identifying challenges and engineering innovative solutions to overcome them.
- ***Practicality***: Focuses on creating tangible, functional, and often groundbreaking products or technologies.
- ***Curiosity***: Driven by a deep desire to understand how things work and to explore new possibilities.
- ***Persistence***: Often dedicated and tenacious, working tirelessly to bring their inventions to life and perfect their designs.

The **Inventor** is often depicted in literature, film, and popular culture as a character who develops groundbreaking technologies, innovative solutions to real-world problems, pioneers new industries or fields of study, uses their inventive skills to save the day.

This archetype highlights the human capacity to overcome challenges and produce transformative change through the creation of approaches, technologies, and solutions.

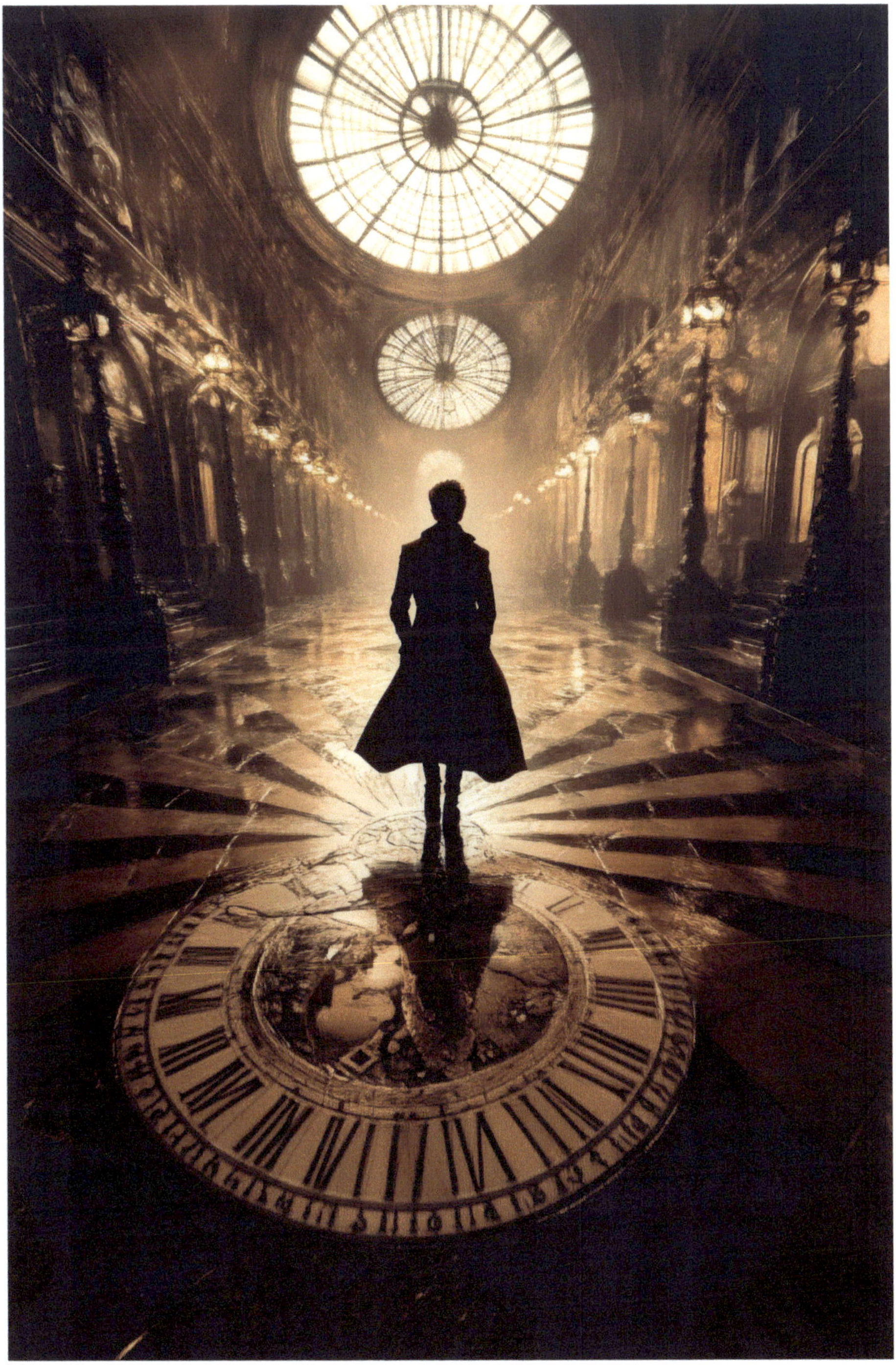

The Lone Wolf Archetype

The Lone Wolf represents individuals who stand apart from society, preferring solitude or operating outside of conventional norms. This archetype is characterized by:

- ***Independence***: A strong preference for autonomy and self-reliance.
- ***Nonconformity***: A tendency to reject or question societal expectations and rules.
- ***Isolation***: often self-imposed, separating themselves from groups or communities.
- ***Self-sufficiency***: Resourcefulness and the ability to thrive without the support of others.
- ***Mystique***: Often perceived as enigmatic, mysterious, or even threatening by those around them.

The **Lone Wolf** is common in stories, films, and literature, depicting characters who operate on the fringes of society, such as rebels, outlaws, or solitary heroes.

This archetype explores themes of individualism, the human need for connection, and the tension between personal freedom and belonging.

Examples include the ***Man with No Name*** from Sergio Leone's spaghetti westerns, ***Lisbeth Salander*** from The Girl with the Dragon Tattoo, and numerous other characters who embody the spirit of the outsider.

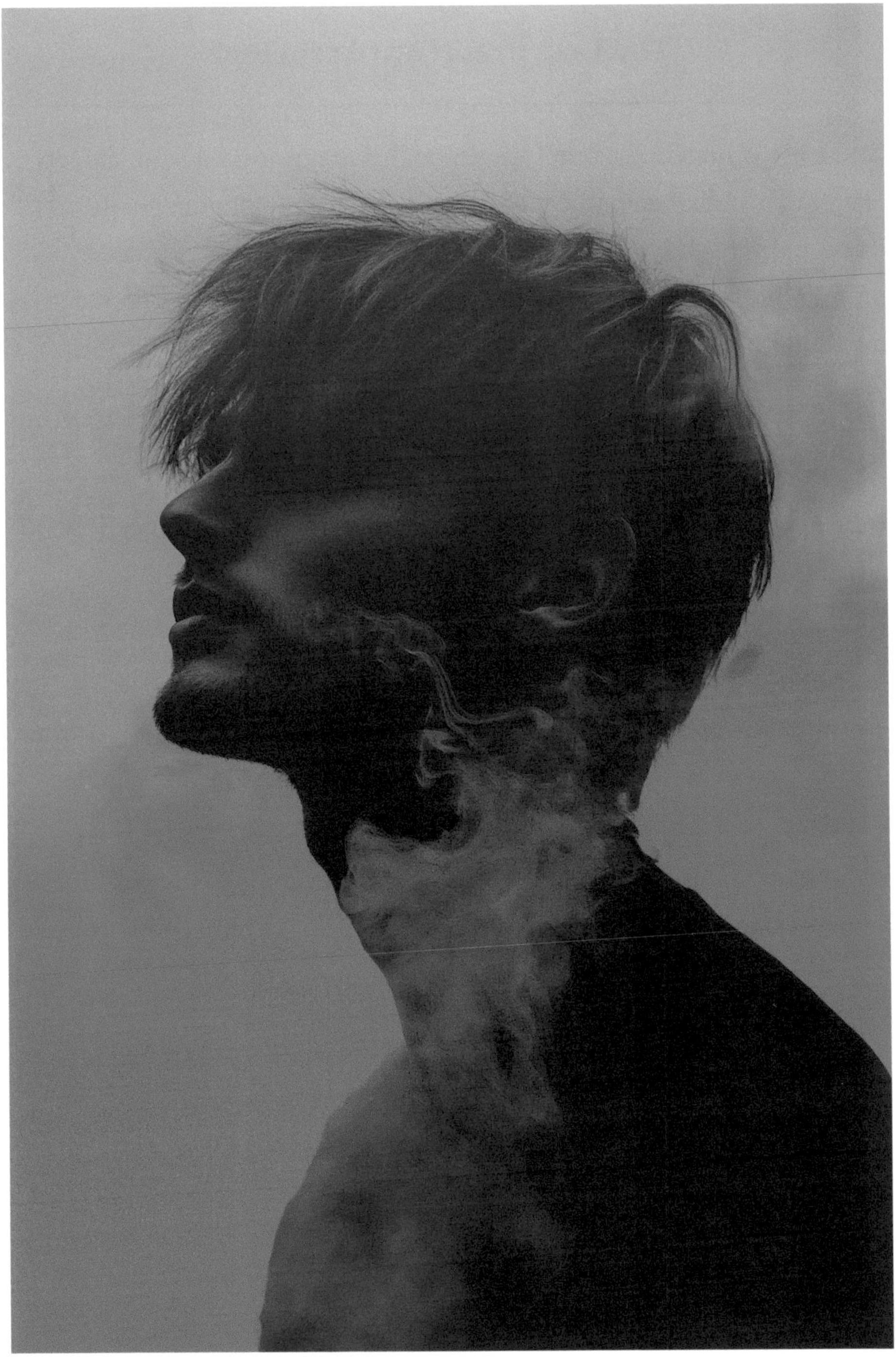

The Lost Innocence Archetype

The Lost Innocence Archetype embodies the transition from naivety and purity to disillusionment and a harsh awakening to the realities of the world. This archetype represents individuals who experience a profound loss of innocence, often through traumatic events, betrayals, or the shattering of illusions. Key characteristics include:

- ***Naivety***: Begins with a sense of innocence, trust, and an idealized view of the world.
- ***Disillusionment***: Experiences a jarring awakening to the harsh realities of life, often involving pain, suffering, or injustice.
- ***Loss***: Confronts the loss of childhood, trust, or ideals, leading to a sense of grief and disenchantment.
- ***Transformation***: Undergoes a significant change in perspective, often becoming more cynical, world-weary, or determined to bring about change.
- ***Wisdom***: Gains a deeper understanding of the complexities of life, human nature, and the world, though often at a great personal cost.

Lost Innocence is often depicted in literature, film, and cultural narratives as characters who undergo a dramatic shift from innocence to experience, such as **Pip** in Charles Dickens' Great Expectations and **Holden Caulfield** in J.D. Salinger's The Catcher in the Rye

This archetype highlights the human experience of disillusionment, the pain of lost innocence, and the potential for personal growth and transformation through confronting the harsh realities of life.

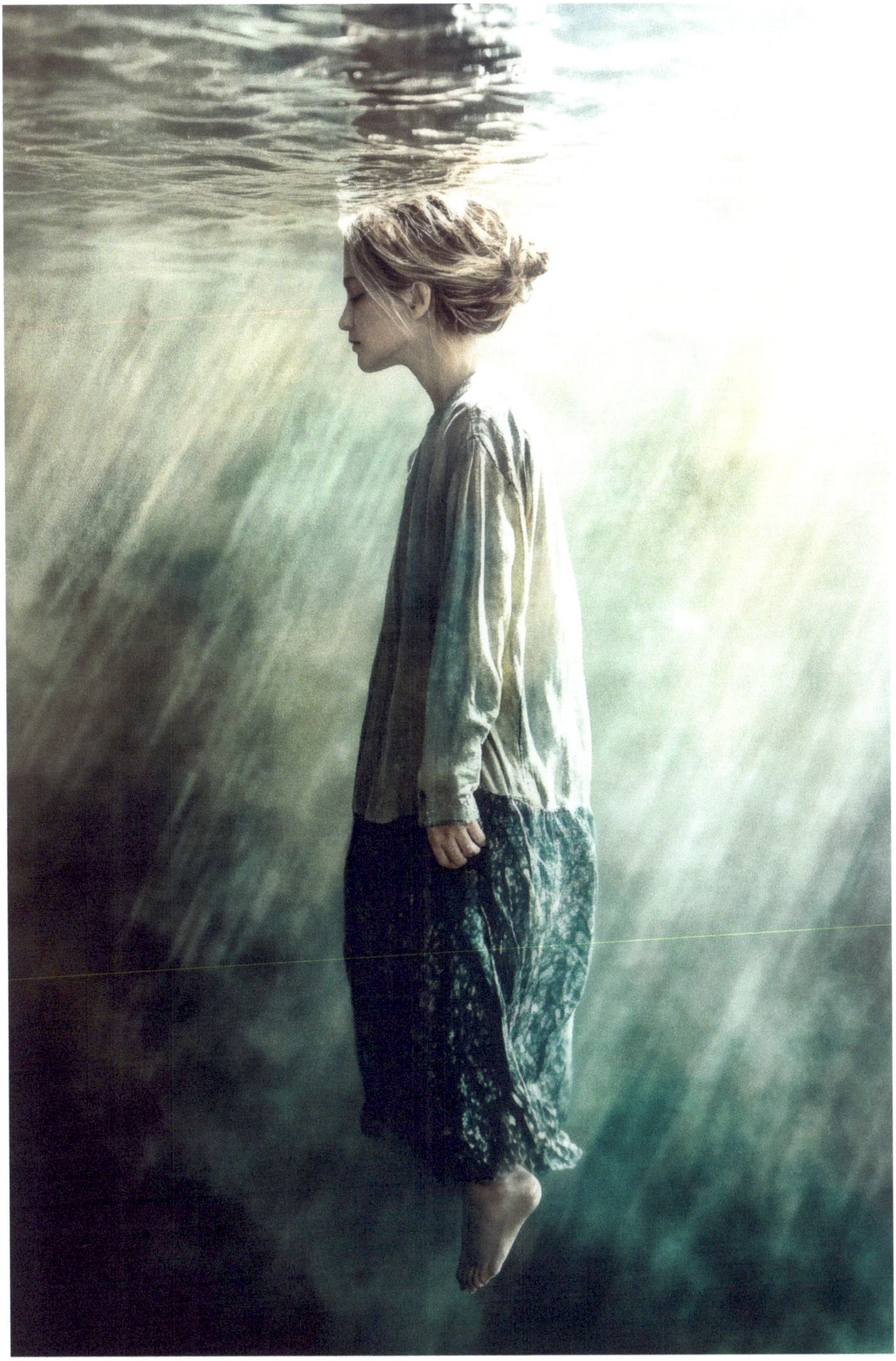

The Lover Archetype

The Lover Archetype embodies passion, intimacy, and the pursuit of emotional connection and sensual pleasure. This archetype represents individuals who are driven by a desire for love, closeness, and the appreciation of beauty and sensory experiences. Key characteristics of this archetype include:

- ***Passionate***: Experiences deep, intense emotions and a strong desire for romantic and sensual experiences.
- ***Empathetic***: Highly attuned to the emotions and needs of others, often prioritizing harmony and connection in relationships.
- ***Appreciative***: Finds joy and fulfillment in the beauty of the world, whether in nature, art, or other sensory experiences.
- ***Sensual***: Enjoys indulging in pleasures that engage the senses, such as fine food, luxurious surroundings, and physical intimacy.
- ***Devoted***: Committed to nurturing and maintaining strong, meaningful relationships with others.

The **Lover** is often depicted in literature, film, and cultural narratives as romantic figures, devoted partners, and individuals who embody the ideals of love and passion.

Examples include characters like **Romeo and Juliet**, **Elizabeth Bennet** and **Mr. Darcy** from Pride and Prejudice, and other iconic lovers who embody the depth and complexity of emotional connection. This archetype highlights the human desire for love, intimacy, and the pursuit of sensual and emotional fulfillment.

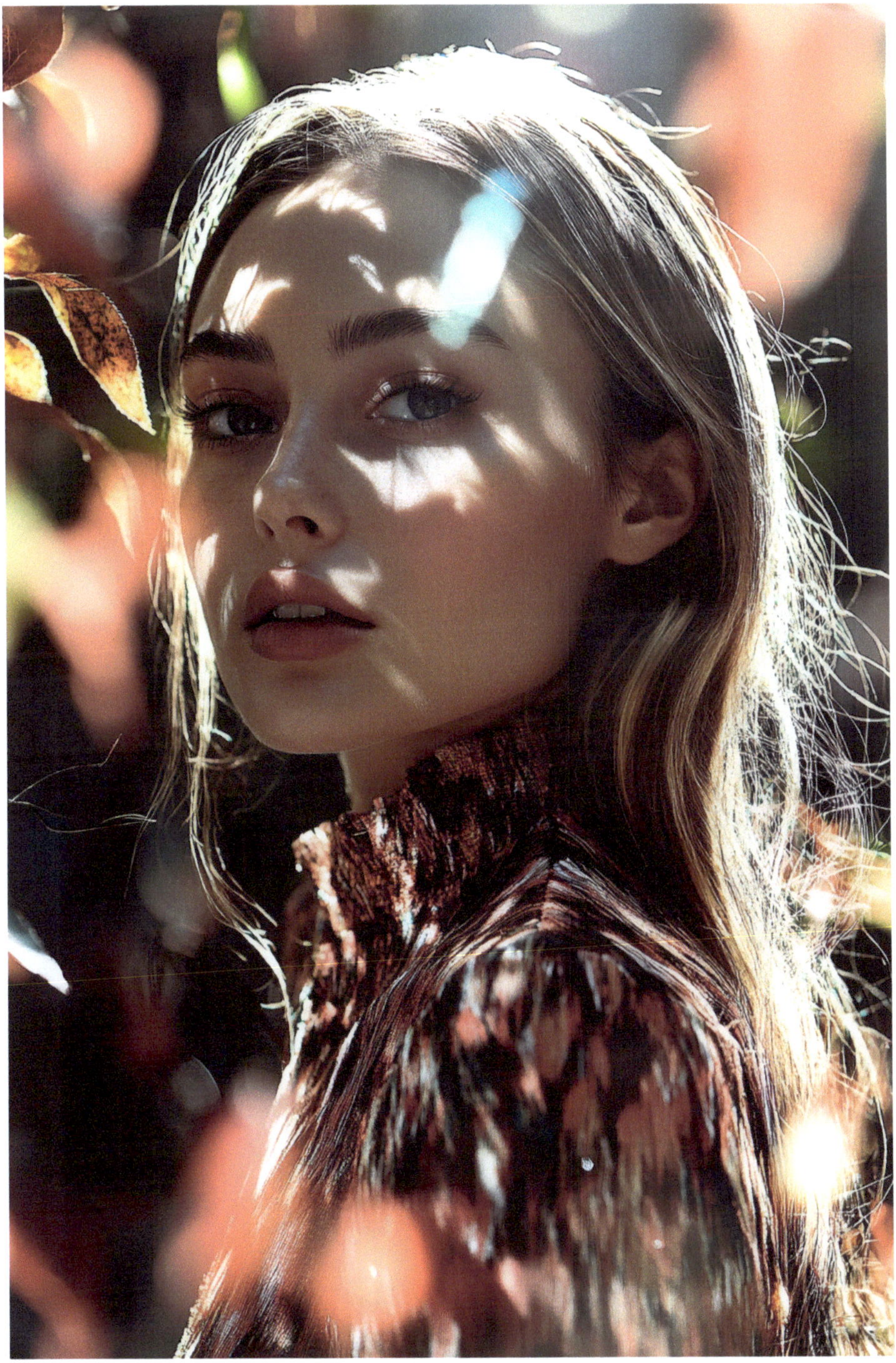

The Magician Archetype

The Magician Archetype embodies transformation, mystical insight, and the ability to influence or control aspects of reality through extraordinary means. This archetype represents individuals who possess hidden knowledge, spiritual wisdom, or supernatural abilities, using them to bring about change and achieve their goals. Key characteristics of the archetype include:

- ***Mystical***: Connected to the spiritual or supernatural realm, often possessing esoteric knowledge or abilities.
- ***Transformative***: Able to bring about significant changes, whether in themselves, others, or the world around them.
- ***Visionary***: Sees beyond the ordinary, perceiving hidden truths, possibilities, or futures.
- ***Charismatic***: Often possesses a captivating presence, inspiring awe, fascination, or even fear in others.
- ***Manipulative***: May use their powers to influence or control people, events, or the environment, sometimes for personal gain.

The **Magician** is often depicted in myths, literature, and popular culture as sorcerers, witches, spiritual gurus, or other figures who wield extraordinary powers. Examples include characters like **Merlin** from Arthurian legend, **Gandalf** from The Lord of the Rings, and the enigmatic, charismatic figures found in various narratives. This archetype highlights the human fascination with the mystical, the potential for personal transformation, and the complex interplay between power, wisdom, and responsibility.

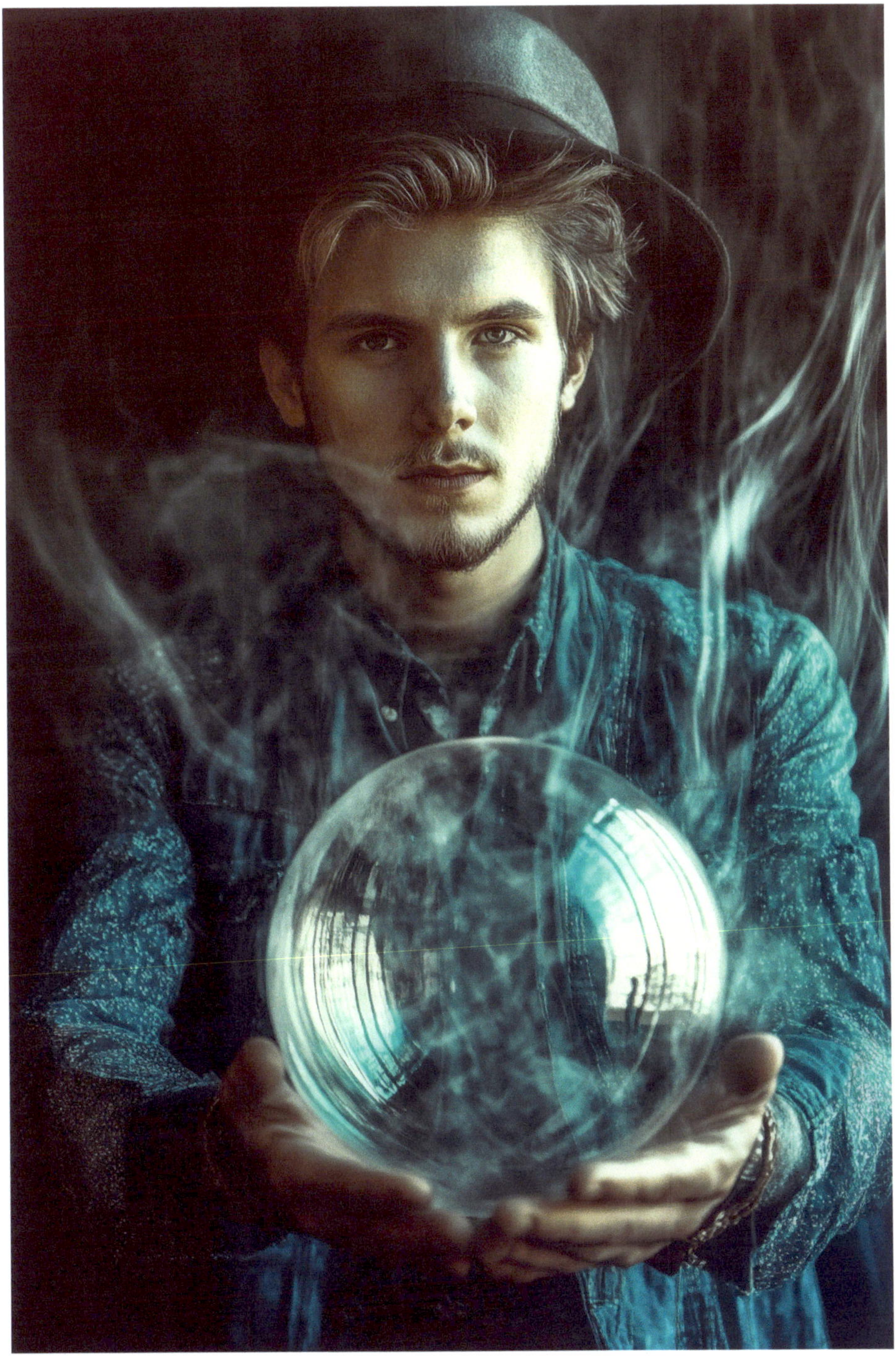

The Mask Archetype

The Mask Archetype represents the facades or false personas that individuals adopt to conceal their true selves, protect their vulnerabilities, or meet societal expectations. This archetype explores the dichotomy between one's authentic identity and the public image they present to the world. Key aspects include:

- ***Deception***: Presenting a false or misleading appearance to hide true feelings, thoughts, or intentions.
- ***Protection***: Using the mask as a defense mechanism to shield oneself from emotional harm or judgment.
- ***Adaptation***: Changing one's behavior or appearance to fit in with different social situations or expectations.
- ***Duality***: The struggle between the authentic self and the public persona, often leading to inner conflict or a desire to be truly seen and understood.

The **Mask** is prevalent in stories, films, and literature, depicting characters who wear metaphorical or literal masks to hide their true identities, such as superheroes with secret identities, undercover agents, or individuals concealing their authentic selves due to fear or shame. This archetype highlights the human tendency to present a filtered or idealized version of oneself to the world, and the complex interplay between authenticity and social expectations. Examples include characters like ***Bruce Wayne/Batman***, ***Don Diego de la Vega/Zorro***, and numerous other figures who embody the concept of the mask.

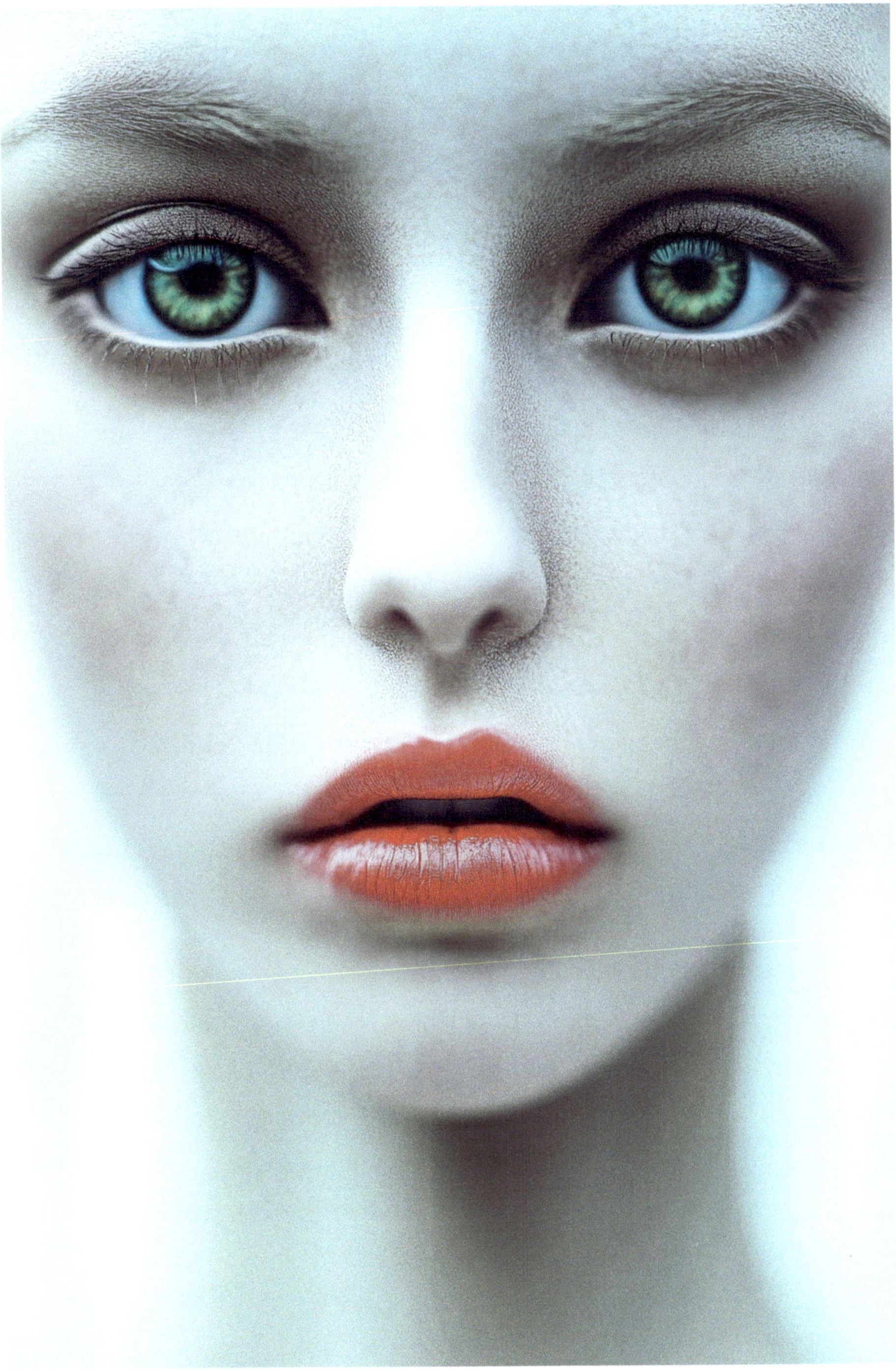

The Mentor Archetype

The Mentor Archetype embodies guidance, wisdom, and the nurturing of potential in others. This archetype represents experienced, knowledgeable, or insightful individuals who support, advise, and inspire their protégés to grow, learn, and achieve their goals. Key characteristics include:

- ***Wisdom***: Possesses valuable knowledge, experience, or insights, often gained through years of practice or personal journey.
- ***Guidance***: Offers advice, support, and encouragement, helping their protégés navigate challenges, make decisions, and stay on their path.
- ***Nurturing***: Fosters the growth and development of their protégés, often serving as a role model, teacher, or confidant.
- ***Patience***: Understands that growth and learning take time, providing steady support through the ups and downs of their protégé's journey.
- ***Selflessness***: Prioritizes their protégé's needs, often putting their own interests aside to focus on their mentee's success and well-being.

The **Mentor** is often depicted in literature, film, and popular culture as: wise, experienced teachers or trainers who help their students or apprentices develop skills, gain knowledge, or find their way; supportive, nurturing figures who provide emotional guidance and encouragement; characters who offer spiritual or philosophical insights, helping their protégés find meaning, purpose, or enlightenment.

This archetype highlights the potential for growth and transformation through supportive, nurturing relationships.

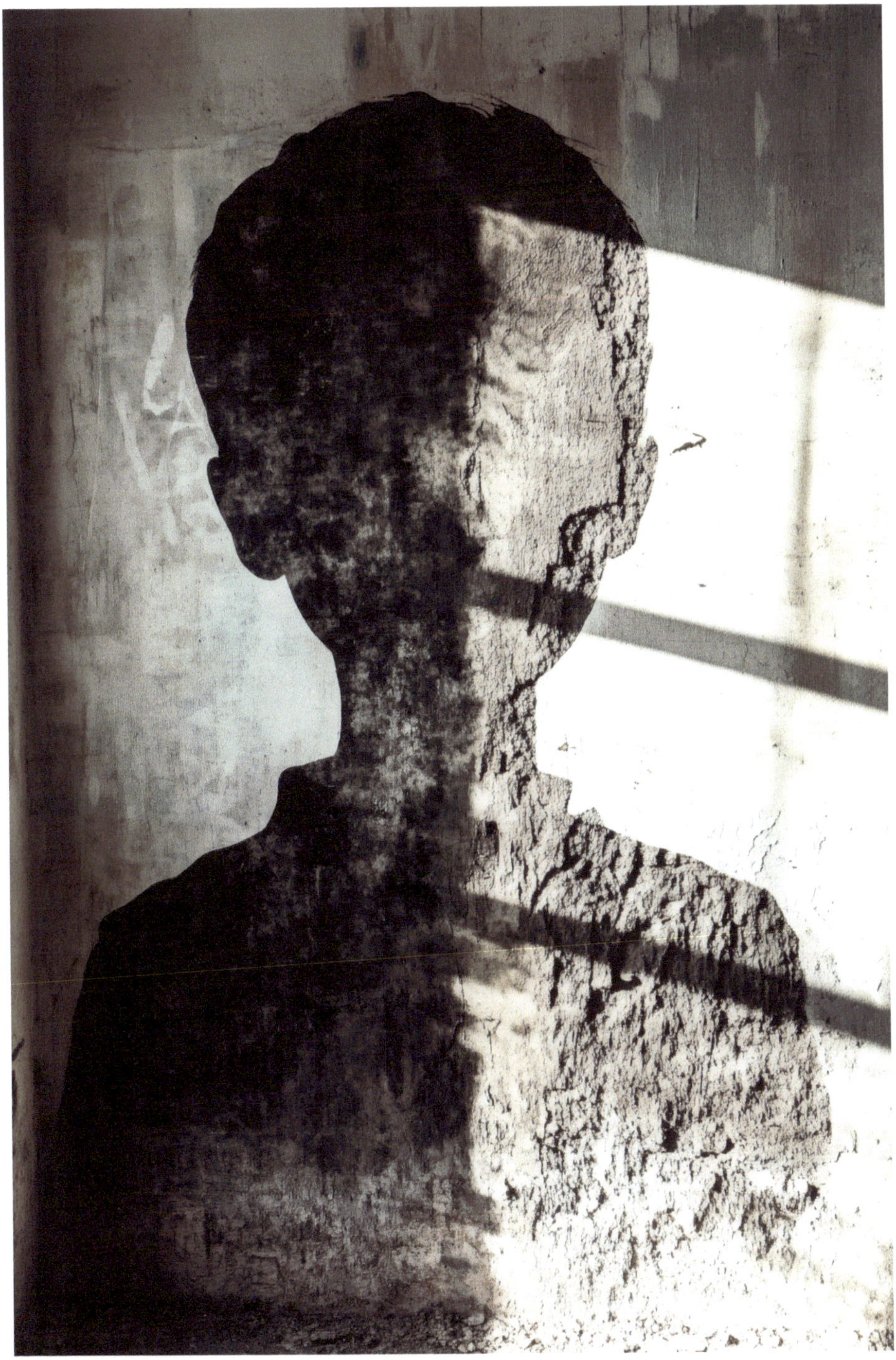

The Moon as a Female Archetype

The Moon as a Female Archetype embodies intuition, emotion, and the cyclical nature of life and fertility. This archetype represents the feminine principles of nurturing, adaptation, and mystery, often serving as a symbol of the divine feminine or the inner world of feelings and unconscious thoughts. Key characteristics include:

- ***Intuition***: Represents the intuitive, instinctual aspects of the feminine, guiding through emotion, empathy, and inner knowing.
- ***Emotion***: Symbolizes the ebb and flow of feelings, reflecting the emotional landscape and the capacity for nurturing, compassion, and sensitivity.
- ***Cycles***: Embodies the cyclical nature of life, fertility, and renewal, mirroring the phases of the moon and the menstrual cycle, as well as the cycles of birth, death, and rebirth.
- ***Mystery***: Evokes the enigmatic, elusive, or hidden qualities of the feminine, often associated with the unconscious mind, dreams, and the unknown.
- ***Adaptability***: Represents the capacity to change, adapt, and transform, reflecting the moon's changing phases and the feminine ability to evolve and grow.

The **Moon as a Female** is depicted in mythology, art, and culture as lunar deities or goddesses; as a symbol of love, romance, and the emotional landscape; and as a representation of the feminine psyche, dreams, and the unconscious mind, often explored in psychological theories and spiritual practices.

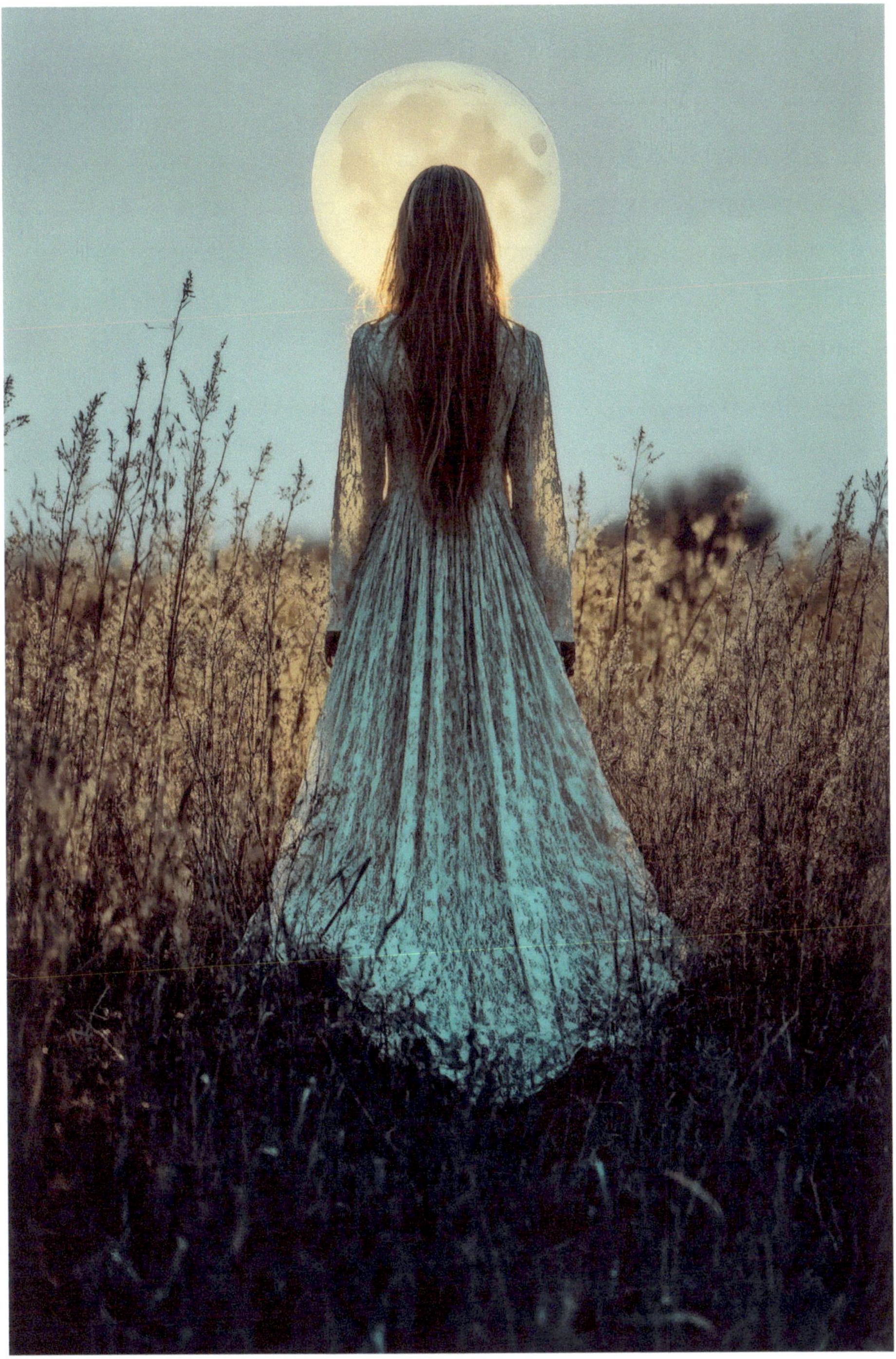

The Misfit Archetype

The Misfit Archetype embodies nonconformity, alienation, and a sense of not belonging to conventional society or groups. This archetype represents individuals who stand apart from the mainstream, either by choice or because they are shunned or excluded. Key characteristics of the Misfit include:

- ***Nonconformity***: Rejects or does not adhere to societal norms, expectations, or conventions.
- ***Alienation***: Feels isolated, disconnected, or out of place in social situations or communities.
- ***Independence***: Often values individuality and personal freedom over fitting in or belonging.
- ***Critical***: May question or challenge established beliefs, systems, or authorities.
- ***Marginalized***: Sometimes pushed to the fringes of society due to their unique qualities, beliefs, or behaviors.

The **Misfit** is often depicted in literature, film, and cultural narratives as rebels, outcasts, or eccentric characters who struggle to find their place in the world. Examples include characters like **Holden Caulfield** from The Catcher in the Rye, the **Phantom of the Opera**, and other figures who embody the complexities and challenges of not fitting in. This archetype highlights the human experiences of alienation, the tension between individuality and belonging, and the potential for personal growth and transformation through embracing one's unique identity.

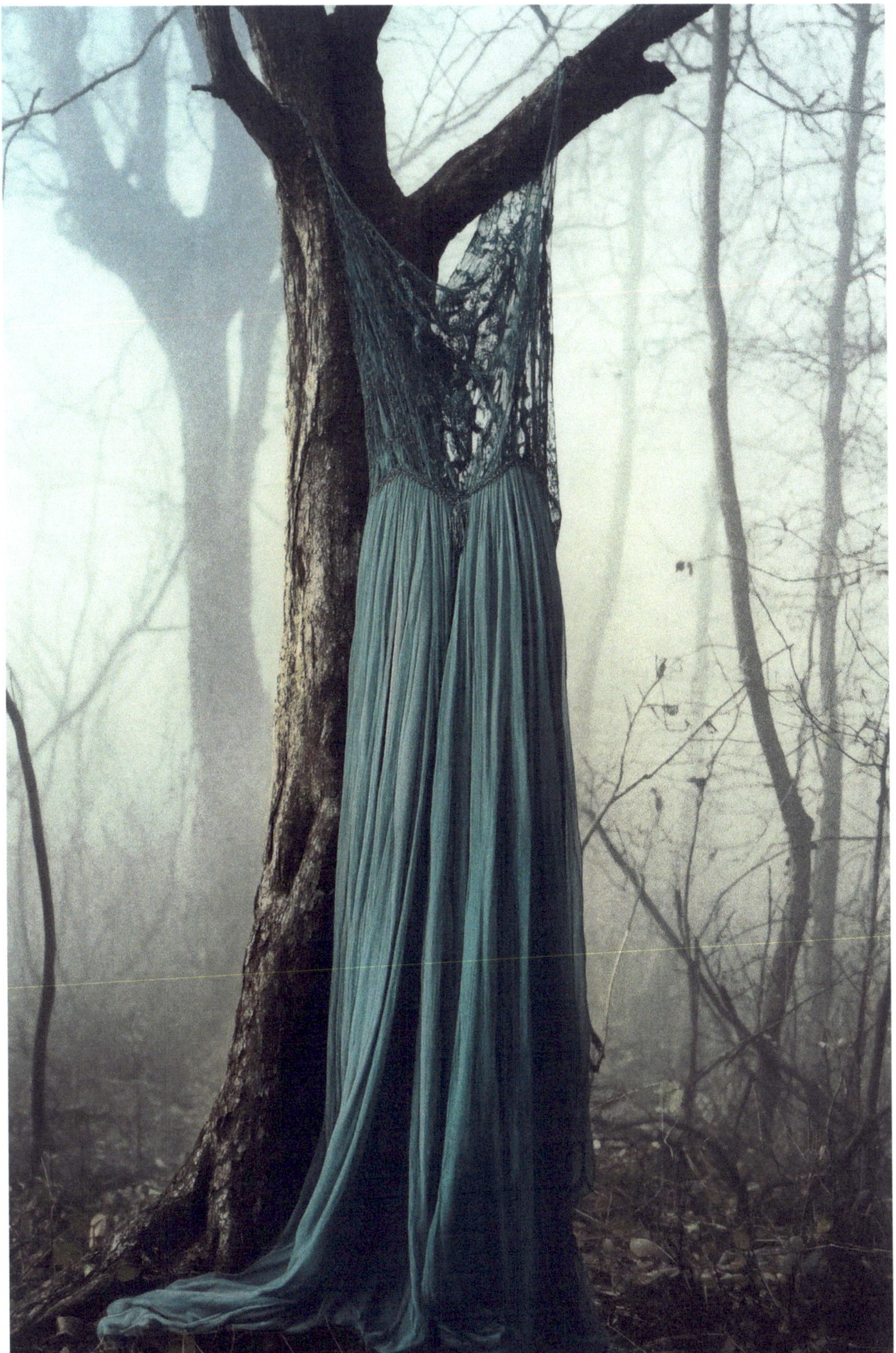

The Mystic/Seeker Archetype

The Mystic/Seeker Archetype embodies the pursuit of spiritual enlightenment, transcendent experiences, and a deep connection to the divine or the unknown. This archetype represents individuals who are driven by a profound desire to understand the mysteries of life, the universe, and their place within it. Key characteristics include:

- ***Spiritual Quest***: Engaged in a journey to find spiritual truth, enlightenment, or union with the divine.
- ***Introspection***: Deeply focused on inner exploration, meditation, and self-discovery.
- ***Transcendence***: Seeks experiences that go beyond the ordinary, often involving altered states of consciousness or mystical encounters.
- ***Asceticism***: May embrace a simple, disciplined lifestyle to facilitate spiritual growth and detachment from material concerns.
- ***Wisdom***: Often gains profound insights and understanding through their spiritual pursuits, which they may share with others.

The **Mystic/Seeker** is often depicted in religious and spiritual narratives, as well as in literature and film, through characters such as spiritual teachers, wandering ascetics, and individuals on quests for enlightenment. Examples include figures like **Buddha**, **St. Francis of Assisi**, and characters in stories that explore spiritual journeys and the search for meaning. This archetype highlights the human yearning for spiritual connection, the pursuit of transcendent experiences, and the quest for ultimate truth and understanding.

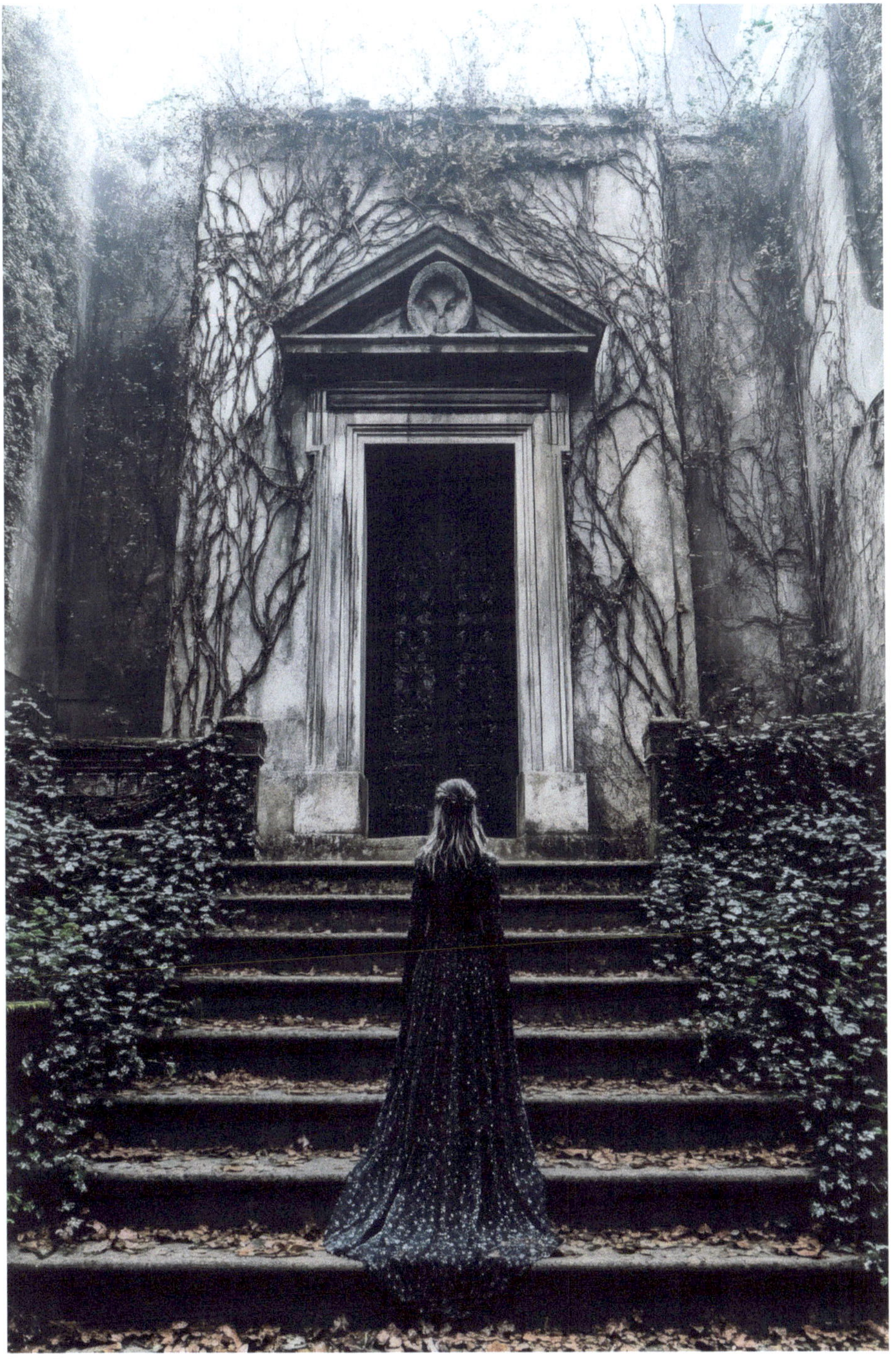

The Nature vs. Technology Duality

The Nature vs. Technology Duality represents the tension and often conflicting relationship between the natural world and technological advancements. This duality explores the balance, opposition, or integration of organic, ecological systems with artificial, man-made innovations. Key aspects include:

- ***Conflict***: The struggle between the preservation of nature and the pursuit of technological progress, often highlighting the environmental impact of industry and innovation.
- ***Balance***: The search for harmony and coexistence between natural ecosystems and technological developments, promoting sustainability and responsible innovation.
- ***Contrast***: The juxtaposition of organic, living systems with mechanical, artificial constructs, emphasizing the differences in aesthetics, functions, and values.
- ***Integration***: The fusion of nature and technology, exploring ways to combine or mimic natural processes and designs in technological applications, such as biomimicry or green technology.
- ***Caution***: The examination of the potential consequences and ethical implications of technological advancements on the natural world and human society.

This duality highlights the human struggle to reconcile the benefits and drawbacks of technological progress with the preservation and appreciation of the natural world.

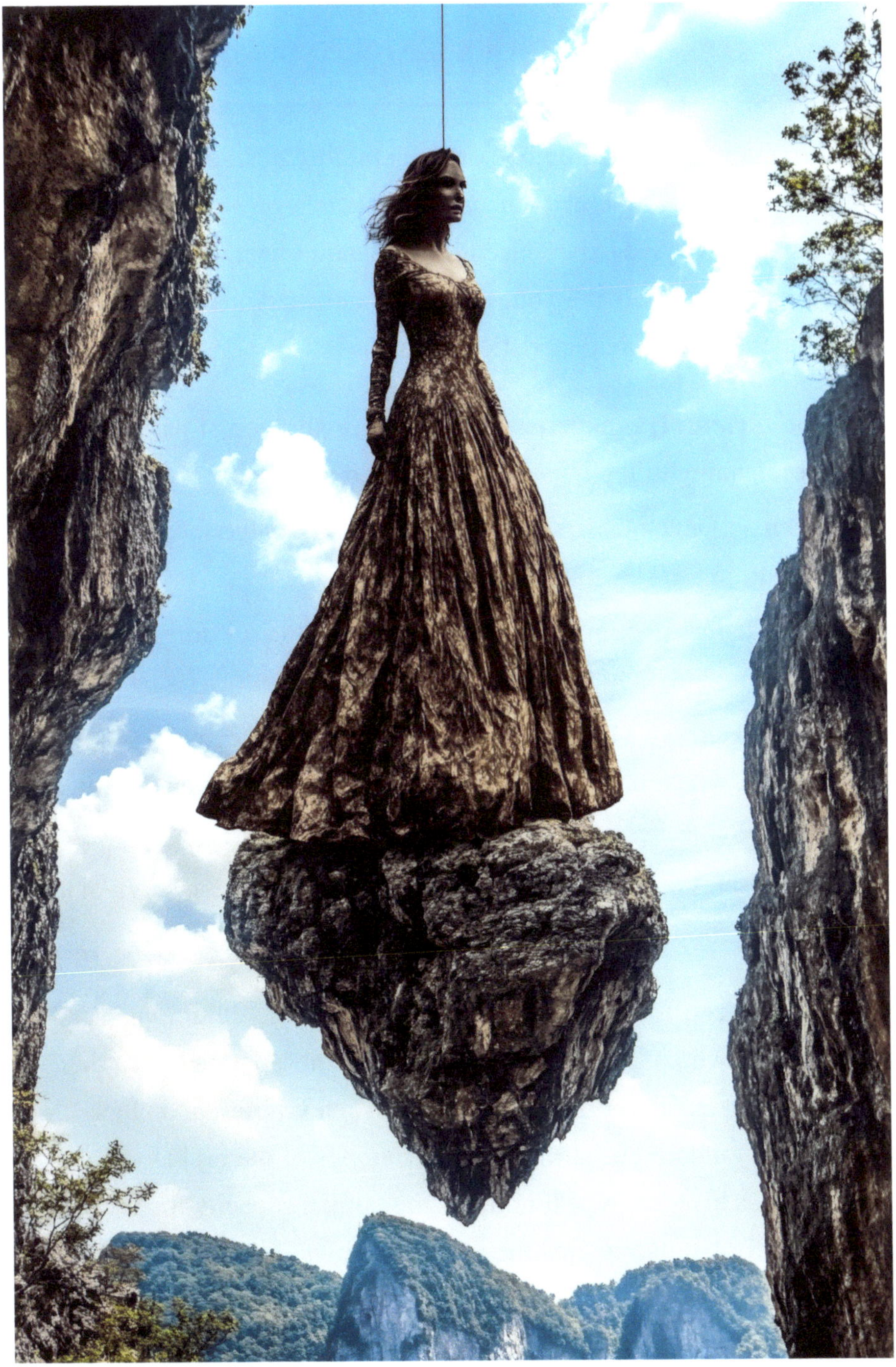

The Orphan Archetype

The Orphan Archetype embodies vulnerability, resilience, and a deep longing for belonging and connection. This archetype represents individuals who have experienced loss, abandonment, or separation from their roots, often at a young age, and must navigate the world independently. Key characteristics include:

- ***Abandonment***: Has experienced the loss or absence of parental figures, leading to feelings of isolation and a search for belonging.
- ***Resilience***: Develops strength and adaptability in the face of adversity, often learning to rely on oneself.
- ***Independence***: Becomes self-reliant and resourceful, forging their own path and making their own decisions.
- ***Longing***: Harbors a deep desire for connection, love, and a sense of belonging, which may manifest as a search for a surrogate family or community.
- ***Pragmatism***: Often grounded and practical, focusing on survival and the present moment rather than dwelling on the past.

The **Orphan** is often depicted in literature, film, and cultural narratives as characters who have lost their parents or been separated from their families, such as **Oliver Twist**, **Anne of Green Gables**, and other figures who embody the struggles and triumphs of the orphan experience. This archetype highlights the human capacity for resilience, the search for belonging, and the personal growth that can emerge from overcoming adversity.

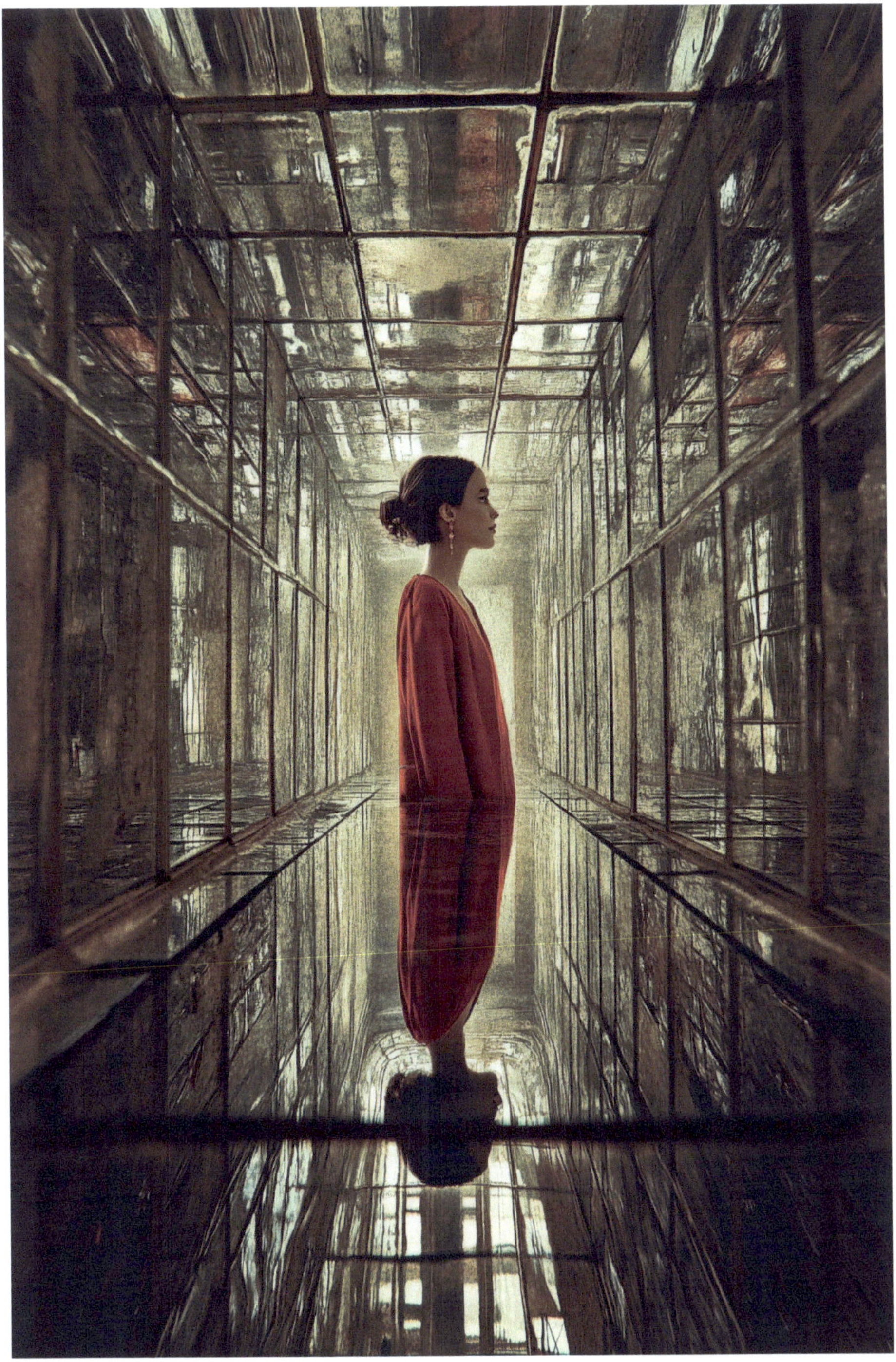

The Outcast Archetype

The Outcast Archetype embodies exclusion, rejection, and a sense of being shunned or pushed to the margins of society. This archetype represents individuals who are ostracized, stigmatized, or deemed unacceptable by the dominant group or community, often leading to feelings of isolation and alienation. Key characteristics include:

- ***Exclusion***: Forcibly removed or distanced from the mainstream, often due to perceived differences, transgressions, or threats to societal norms.
- ***Stigmatization***: Labeled or marked as deviant, inferior, or undesirable, which can lead to prejudice, discrimination, or persecution.
- ***Isolation***: Experiences a sense of separation, loneliness, and disconnection from others, which can foster introspection, resentment, or a desire for revenge.
- ***Nonconformity***: May reject or challenge mainstream values, values, or expectations, sometimes embracing their outsider status as a source of pride or defiance.
- ***Resilience***: Can develop strength, adaptability, and a unique perspective on society, often finding solace, support, or a sense of belonging in alternative communities or subcultures.

The **Outcast** is often depicted in literature, film, and cultural narratives as characters who are shunned, exiled, or vilified, such as **Hester Prynne** in The Scarlet Letter. This archetype highlights the human experiences of rejection, the tension between belonging and otherness,

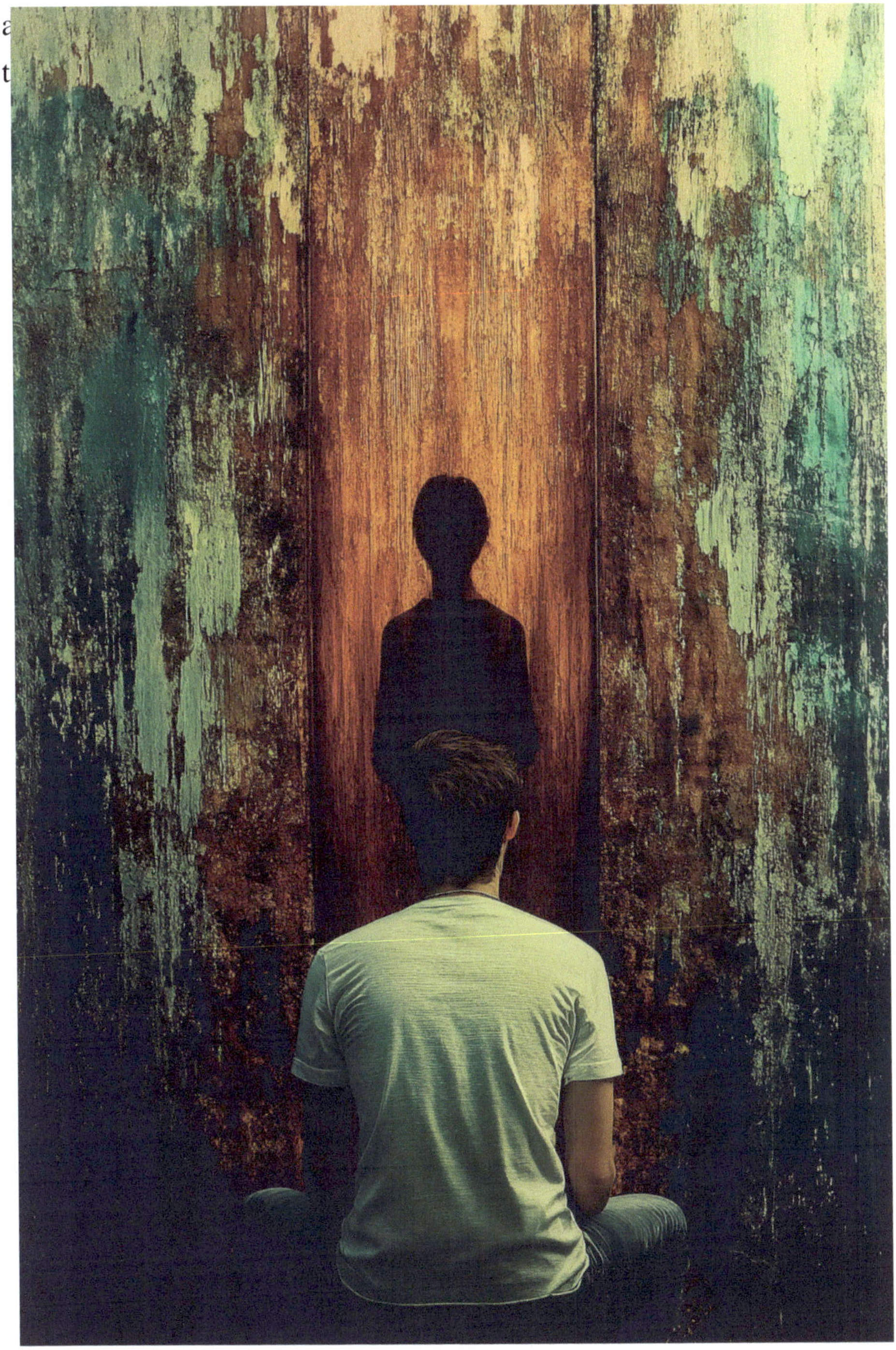

The Outsider Archetype

The Outsider Archetype, similar to the **Misfit**, embodies alienation, detachment, and a sense of not belonging to mainstream society or groups. This archetype represents individuals who are separated from the dominant culture, either voluntarily or involuntarily, often leading to a unique perspective on social dynamics. Key characteristics include:

- ***Detachment***: Stands apart from societal norms, conventions, or expectations, often observing from the periphery.
- ***Alienation***: Feels isolated, disconnected, or estranged from the majority, which can foster a sense of loneliness or independence.
- ***Critical Perspective***: Often possesses a keen, sometimes cynical, insight into the workings of society, questioning or challenging established beliefs and systems.
- ***Independence***: Values personal freedom, autonomy, and the ability to forge one's own path.
- ***Marginalization***: May be excluded, shunned, or pushed to the fringes due to their unique qualities, beliefs, or circumstances.

The **Outsider** is often depicted in literature, film, and cultural narratives as observers, loners, or characters who struggle to find their place in the world. Examples include characters like **Meursault** in Albert Camus' The Stranger, **Nick Carraway** in The Great Gatsby, and other figures who embody the complexities and challenges of being an outsider. This archetype highlights the human experiences of alienation, the tension between belonging and independence, and the potential for unique insights and personal growth through a detached perspective.

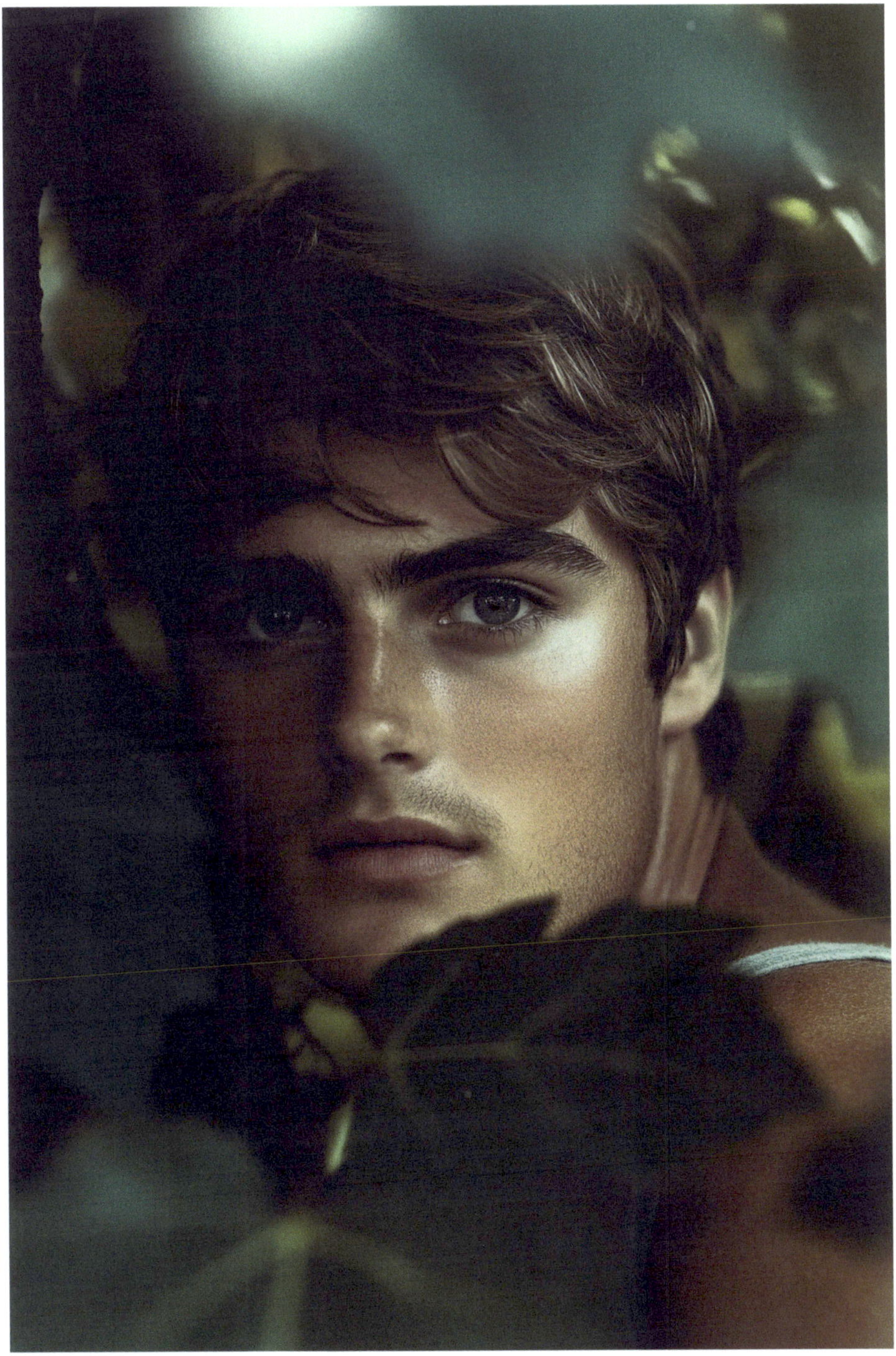

The Otherworldly Archetype

The Otherworldly Archetype embodies the mysterious, ethereal, and supernatural, representing realms, beings, or experiences that transcend the ordinary and familiar. This archetype evokes a sense of wonder, awe, and sometimes unease, as it connects us with the unknown and the intangible. Key characteristics include:

- ***Mystique***: Surrounded by an aura of enigma, magic, or inexplicable phenomena, defying rational explanation.
- ***Transcendence***: Associated with realms or experiences that go beyond the physical world, such as the spiritual, the paranormal, or the fantastical.
- ***Enchantment***: Often inspires a sense of awe, fascination, or entrancing allure, drawing individuals into its captivating realm.
- ***Unpredictability***: Governed by its own rules and logic, often defying the conventions and expectations of the mundane world.
- ***Liminality***: Exists at the threshold or boundary between the known and the unknown, the real and the imagined.

The **Otherworldly** is often depicted in literature, film, and popular culture as magical or fantastical realms, supernatural entities, otherworldly landscapes or phenomena, and haracters or experiences that blur the line between reality and the supernatural.

This archetype highlights the human fascination with the unknown, the allure of the supernatural, and the enduring power of the imagination to conjure realms and experiences that transcend the ordinary.

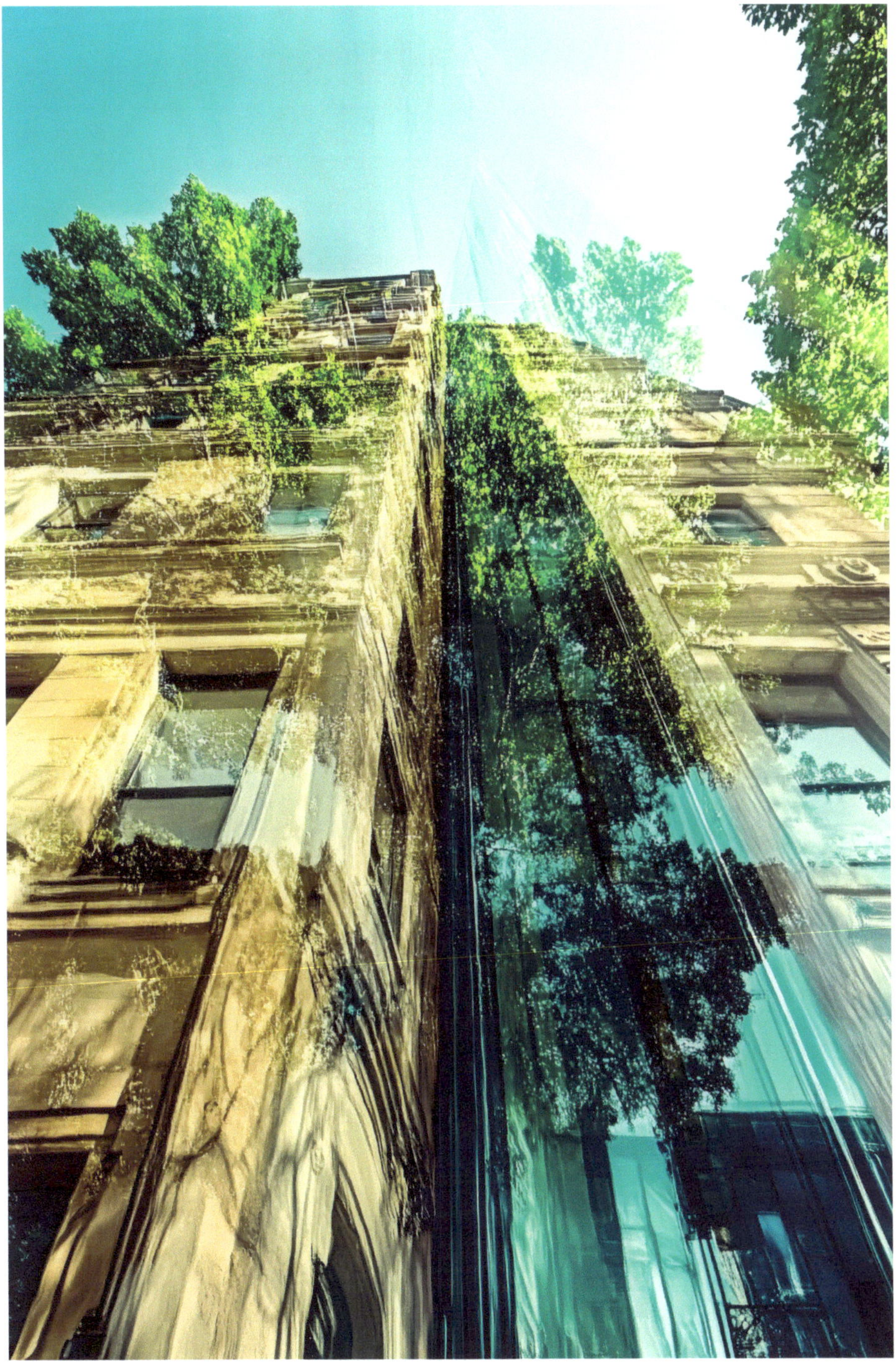

The Persona Archetype

The Persona Archetype, a concept introduced by Carl Jung, represents the social face or public image that an individual presents to the world. It is the consciously constructed identity that reflects how a person wants to be perceived by others, often influenced by societal expectations, cultural norms, and personal aspirations. Key aspects include:

- ***Social Role***: The persona serves as a bridge between the individual's inner self and their social environment, helping them navigate interpersonal interactions and meet societal expectations.
- ***Adaptation***: The persona allows individuals to adapt to different situations and present the most appropriate or desirable aspects of themselves.
- ***Protection***: The persona can act as a defense mechanism, shielding the individual's true feelings, vulnerabilities, or unacceptable impulses from public view.
- ***Aspiration***: The persona often embodies the individual's ego ideal, reflecting their goals, values, and desired qualities.

The **Persona** is evident in various aspects of life, such as the professional roles people adopt, the images they project on social media, and the ways they present themselves in different social contexts.

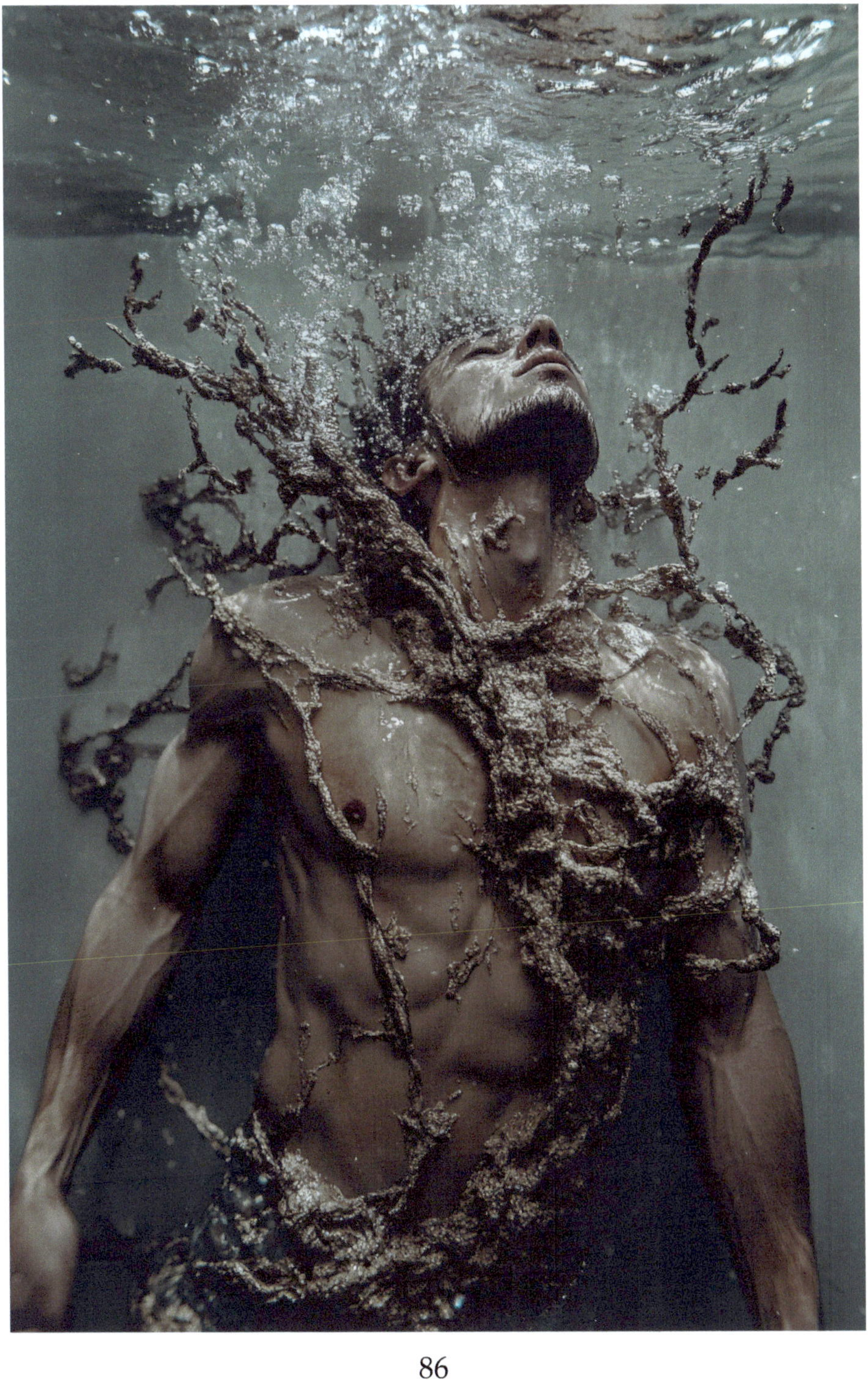

The Pioneer/Trailblazer Archetype

The Pioneer/Trailblazer Archetype embodies innovation, courage, and a drive to venture into uncharted territory, both literally and metaphorically. This archetype represents individuals who forge new paths, challenge conventions, and inspire others to follow their lead. Key characteristics include:

- ***Vision***: Possesses a clear sense of purpose and the ability to see beyond the present, envisioning new possibilities and opportunities.
- ***Courage***: Demonstrates bravery and determination in the face of uncertainty, adversity, or resistance from others.
- ***Independence***: Values autonomy, self-reliance, and the freedom to explore, experiment, and make their own decisions.
- ***Innovation***: Introduces new ideas, methods, or approaches, often disrupting the status quo and driving progress.
- ***Inspiration***: Motivates and encourages others to embrace change, take risks, and pursue their own goals and dreams.

The **Pioneer/Trailblazer** is often depicted in literature, film, and popular culture as explorers and adventurers who journey into unknown lands, entrepreneurs and innovators who revolutionize industries or create groundbreaking products; activists and reformers who challenge societal norms and advocate for change; and artists and creators who push the boundaries of their medium, forging new styles, genres, or forms of expression. This archetype highlights the potential for transformative change through courageous leadership and a willingness to explore new horizons.

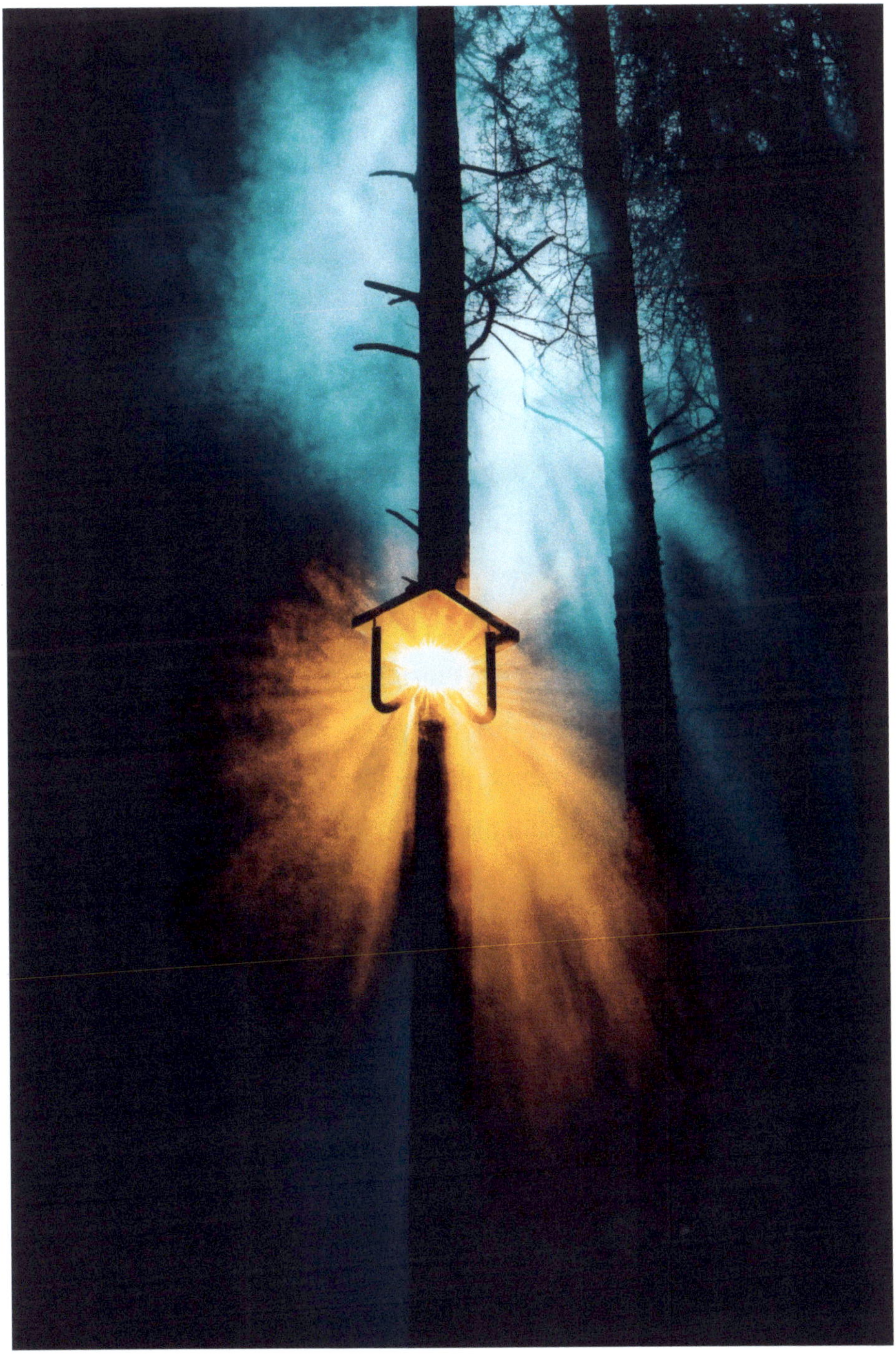

The Philosopher Archetype

The Philosopher Archetype embodies wisdom, contemplation, and the pursuit of deep understanding and truth. This archetype represents individuals who are driven by a desire to question, analyze, and make sense of the world, the human condition, and the fundamental nature of reality. Key characteristics include:

- ***Introspection***: Engages in deep reflection and self-examination to gain insight into the self and the human experience.
- ***Analytical***: Possesses a keen intellect and the ability to dissect complex ideas, arguments, and concepts.
- ***Wisdom***: Seeks or offers profound understanding, knowledge, or enlightenment, often sharing their insights with others.
- ***Truth-seeking***: Driven by a strong desire to uncover and comprehend the essential truths of existence, ethics, and the universe.
- ***Detachment***: Often adopts an objective, impartial perspective, observing and contemplating the world from a distance.

The **Philosopher** is depicted in literature, film, and popular culture as: wise sages, teachers, or mentors who offer guidance and insight; deep thinkers who grapple with existential questions and the meaning of life; characters who embody philosophical ideals or principles; individuals who challenge conventional wisdom, question authority, and provoke thought. This archetype highlights the quest for understanding and the enduring search for wisdom and truth in the face of life's complexities and mysteries.

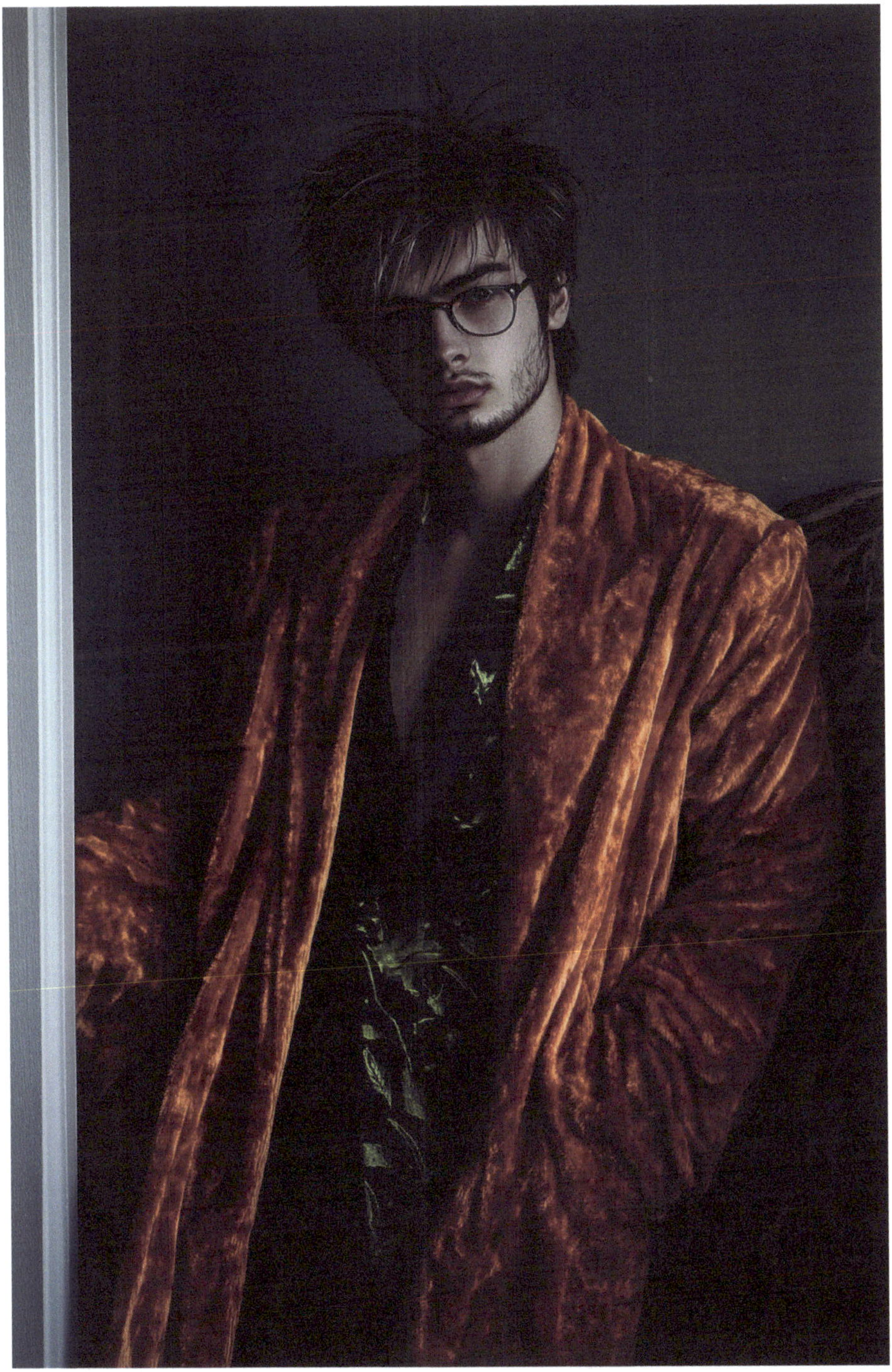

The Primal/Primitive Archetype

The Primal/Primitive Archetype represents the instinctual, untamed, and raw aspects of human nature. This archetype embodies the basic, fundamental forces that drive survival, reproduction, and emotional responses. Key characteristics include:

- ***Instinctual***: Governed by basic urges and impulses, such as hunger, sexual desire, and aggression.
- ***Emotional***: Driven by intense, raw emotions like fear, anger, joy, and passion.
- ***Uncivilized***: Operating outside of societal norms, expectations, and constraints.
- ***Natural***: Closely connected to the natural world and its rhythms.

The **Primal/Primitive** is often depicted in stories, myths, and art as wild beings, savage creatures, or characters who embody the raw, unfiltered aspects of humanity.

Examples include werewolves, primitive deities, and characters like ***Tarzan*** or ***Conan the Barbarian***. This archetype explores the tension between civilization and wildness, as well as the enduring power of instinct and emotion in the human experience.

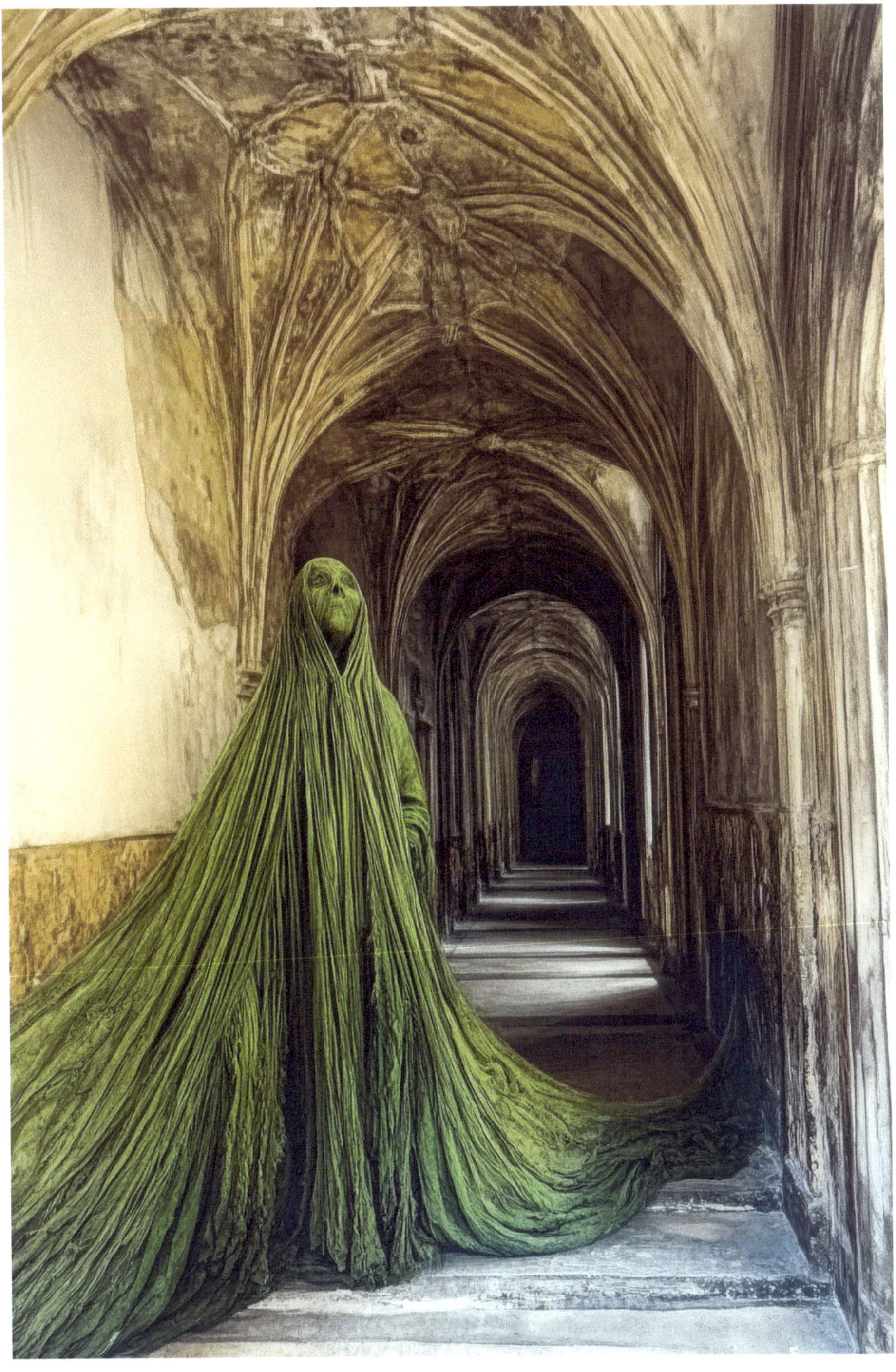

The Quest for Perfection

The Quest for Perfection Archetype represents the relentless pursuit of flawlessness, idealism, and the ultimate achievement of a perfect state. This archetype embodies the human desire to attain the highest standards, overcome all limitations, and reach an idealized version of oneself or the world. Key characteristics include:

- ***Idealism***: A strong focus on achieving an ideal or perfect outcome.
- ***Drive***: An unyielding motivation to improve, excel, and surpass existing standards.
- ***Critical Self-Assessment***: A tendency to scrutinize and evaluate oneself harshly in the pursuit of perfection.
- ***Transformation***: The journey often involves personal growth, self-discovery, and overcoming obstacles to reach the desired state.

The **Quest for Perfection** is often depicted in stories of personal achievement, self-improvement, and the pursuit of excellence. It can be seen in characters who strive for perfection in their craft, seek spiritual enlightenment, or aim to create a utopian society.

This archetype highlights the human aspiration for greatness and the challenges and sacrifices that come with the pursuit of an ideal. Examples include characters like ***Leonardo da Vinci***, athletes striving for gold medals, and protagonists in stories of self-discovery and transformation.

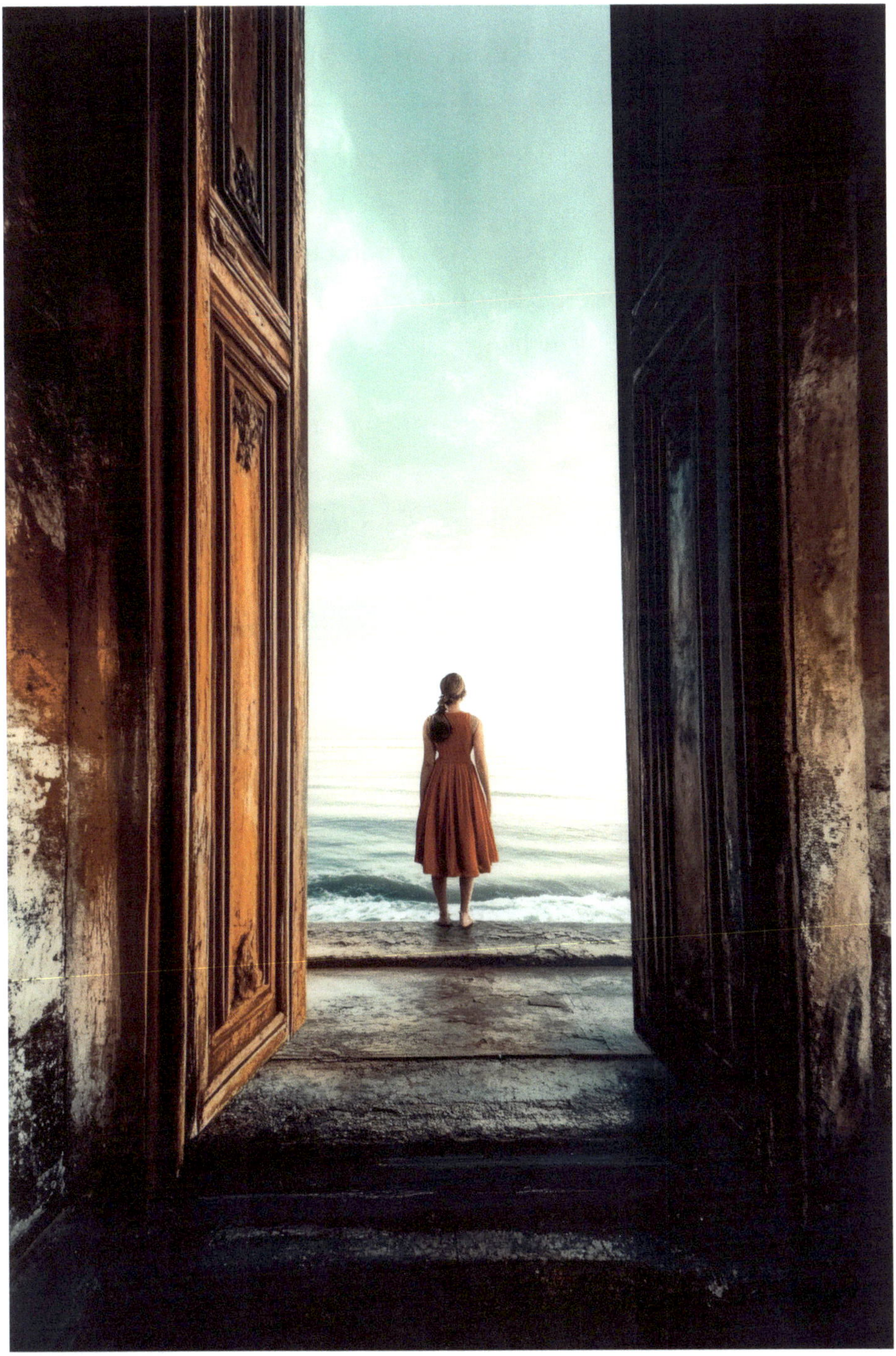

The Rebel Archetype

The Rebel Archetype embodies defiance, nonconformity, and a willingness to challenge or reject established authority, norms, or expectations. This archetype represents individuals who stand against oppression, injustice, or the status quo, often fighting for freedom, individuality, or a cause they believe in. Key characteristics include:

- ***Defiance***: Openly resists, disobeys, or challenges authority figures, rules, or conventions.
- ***Nonconformity***: Rejects or deviates from societal expectations, norms, or traditions, forging their own path and identity.
- ***Passion***: Driven by strong emotions, convictions, or a desire for change, often inspiring others to join their cause.
- ***Courage***: Demonstrates bravery and determination in the face of adversity, opposition, or the risk of personal loss or harm.
- ***Transformation***: Seeks to overthrow, disrupt, or change existing systems, systems, or power structures, often advocating for reform or revolution.

The **Rebel** is often depicted in literature, film, and popular culture as: characters who lead or participate in uprisings, revolutions, or resistance movements; individuals who defy societal expectations or norms; anti-heroes or outlaws who operate outside the law or conventional morality; iconoclasts who challenge or subvert cultural, artistic, or intellectual traditions. This archetype highlights the potential for transformative change through the challenge of authority and the pursuit of personal freedom and justice.

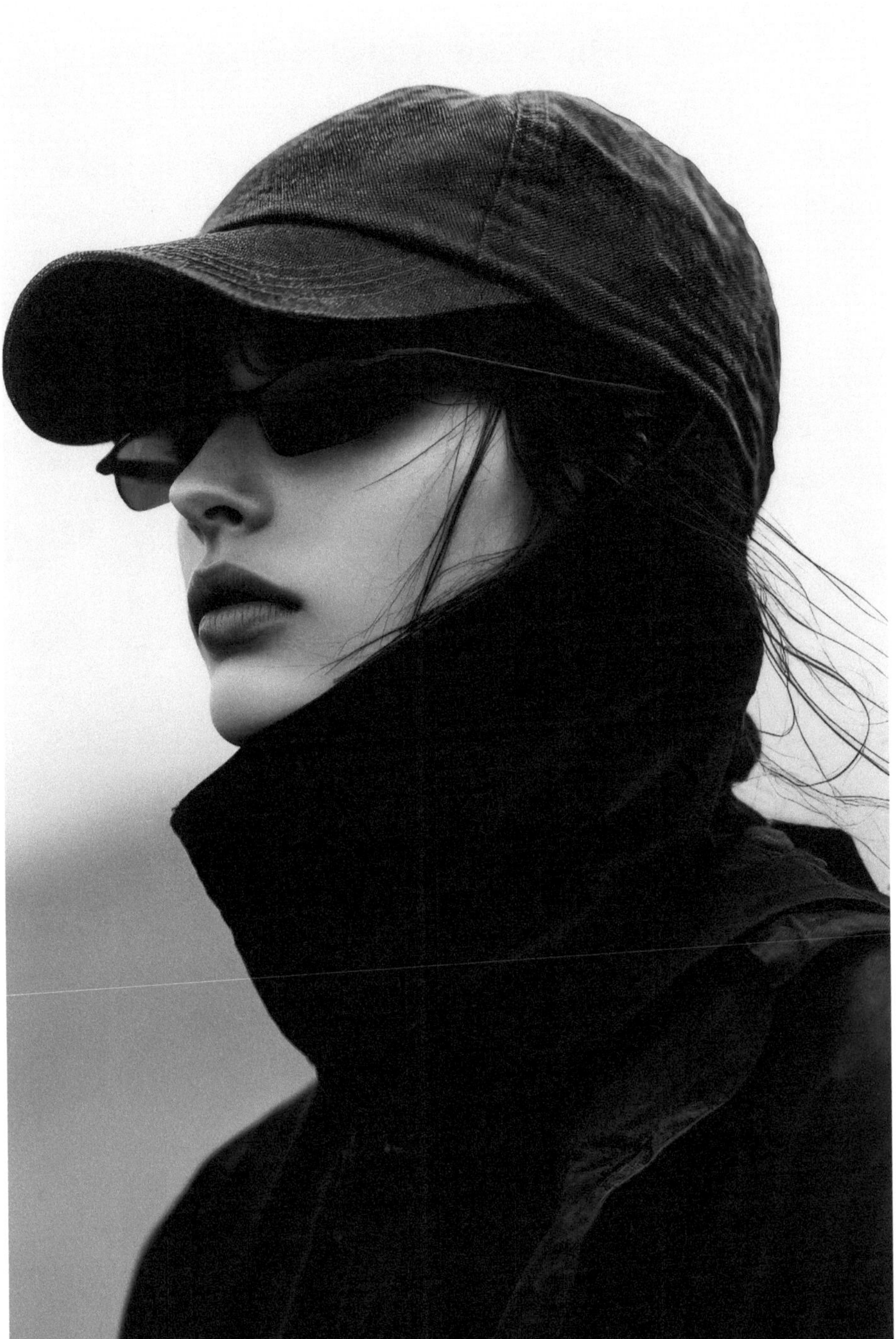

The Ruins as a Symbol of Decay

The Ruins as a Symbol of Decay represent the remnants of once-great structures, civilizations, or ideals that have fallen into disrepair, neglect, or destruction. This symbol embodies the inevitable decline and collapse of man-made creations, the passage of time, and the impermanence of human achievements. Key aspects include:

- ***Decline***: Emphasizes the deterioration and crumbling of physical structures, societies, or beliefs over time.
- ***Mortality***: Serves as a reminder of the transient nature of life and the inescapable reality of death and decay.
- ***Loss***: Conveys a sense of nostalgia, melancholy, or regret for what has been lost, lost potential, or the irretrievable past.
- ***The Past***: Evokes memories or echoes of former glory, historical events, or cultural heritage that have faded or disappeared.
- ***Caution***: Can act as a warning or cautionary tale about the consequences of hubris, neglect, or the cyclical nature of rise and fall.

The **Ruins** are often depicted in literature, art, and cultural narratives as: crumbling buildings, post-apocalyptic landscapes, and the physical or psychological deterioration of characters.

This symbol highlights the human experience of impermanence, the cycle of growth and decay, and the emotional resonance of loss and the passage of time.

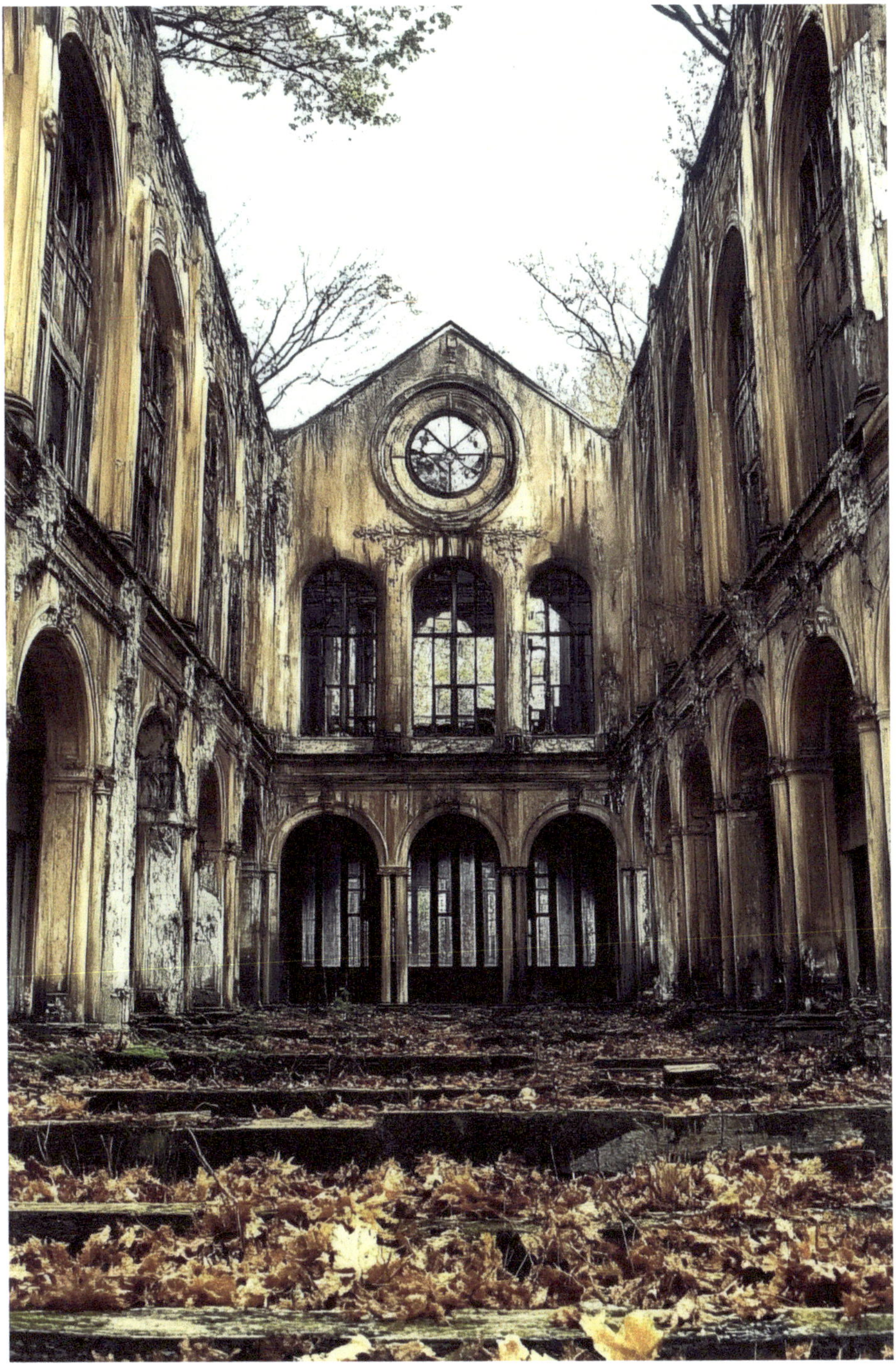

The Sage Archetype

The Sage Archetype represents wisdom, knowledge, and the pursuit of truth. This archetype embodies the seeker and keeper of profound understanding and insight. Key characteristics include:

- ***Wisdom***: Deep understanding and insight gained through experience, reflection, and learning.
- ***Intellectualism***: A strong emphasis on the acquisition and application of knowledge.
- ***Teacher/Mentor***: Often serves as a guide or advisor, sharing wisdom with others.
- ***Reflection***: Values introspection, contemplation, and thoughtful analysis.
- ***Truth-Seeking***: Driven by a desire to uncover and comprehend the fundamental truths of the world.

The **Sage** is often depicted in stories, myths, and cultural narratives as wise old scholars, philosophers, spiritual leaders, or insightful advisors. Examples include characters like ***Gandalf*** from The Lord of the Rings, ***Yoda*** from Star Wars, and historical figures such as ***Socrates*** and ***Confucius***.

This archetype highlights the human quest for understanding, the value of wisdom, and the importance of sharing knowledge with others.

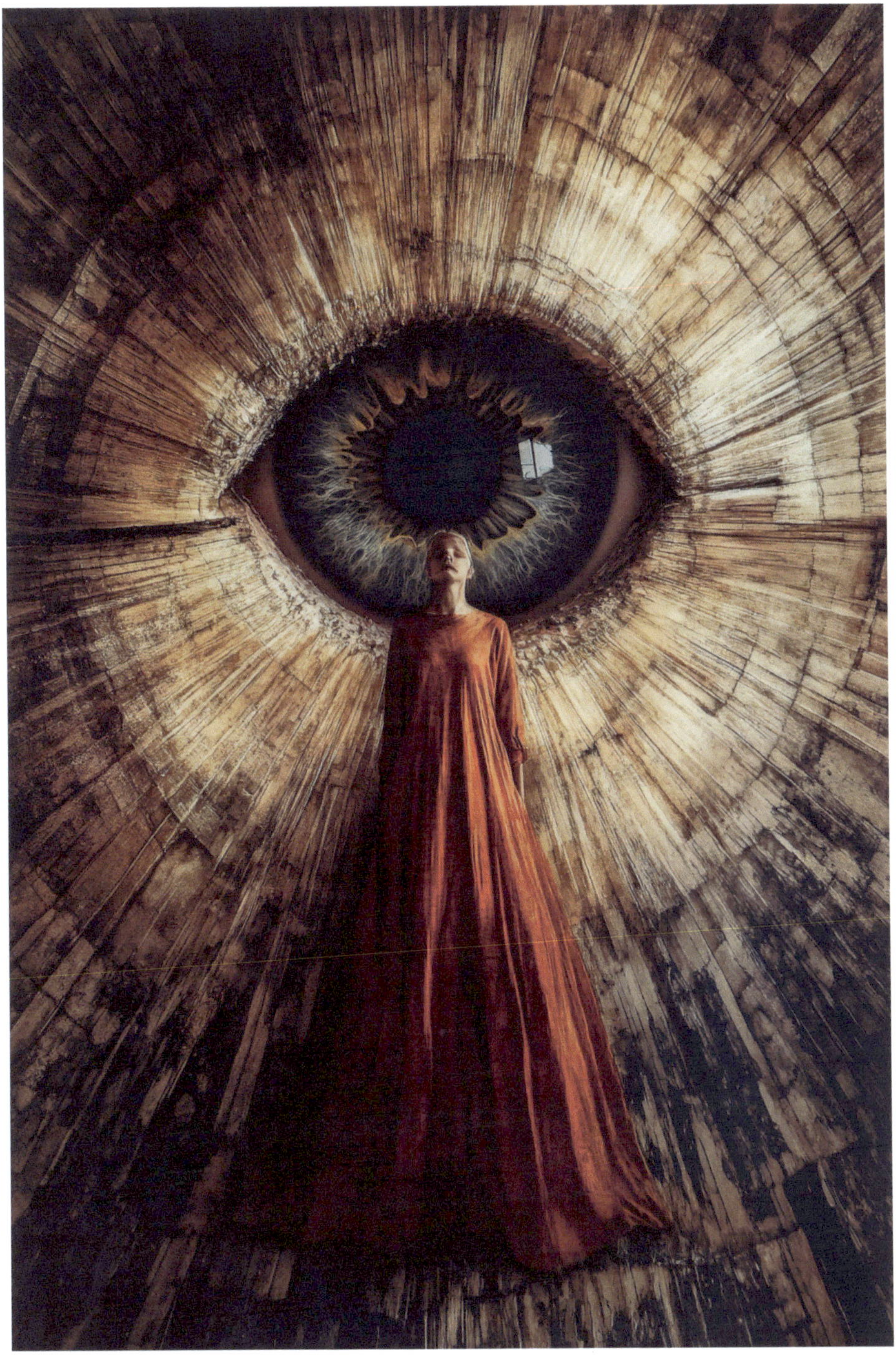

The Seer Archetype

The Seer Archetype embodies intuition, prophetic vision, and the ability to perceive hidden truths or future events. This archetype represents individuals who possess extraordinary insight, foresight, or spiritual awareness, often serving as guides, advisors, or oracles for others. Key characteristics include:

Intuition: Has a keen inner knowing and the ability to sense or perceive information beyond the ordinary senses.

Prophecy: Can foresee future events, trends, or possibilities, often communicating these visions to guide others.

Wisdom: Offers profound insights, advice, or spiritual teachings, helping others to understand complex situations or find their path.

Mysticism: Often connected to the spiritual or otherworldly realms, channeling divine or esoteric knowledge.

Guidance: Acts as a mentor, advisor, or counselor, using their gifts to support and inspire those seeking direction or understanding.

The **Seer** is often depicted in mythology, literature, and popular culture as characters who possess prophetic or oracular abilities, offers wisdom and guidance, has heightened intuition or spiritual awareness, or serves as a spiritual teacher or mentor.

This archetype highlights the human capacity for the perception of hidden truths and future possibilities.

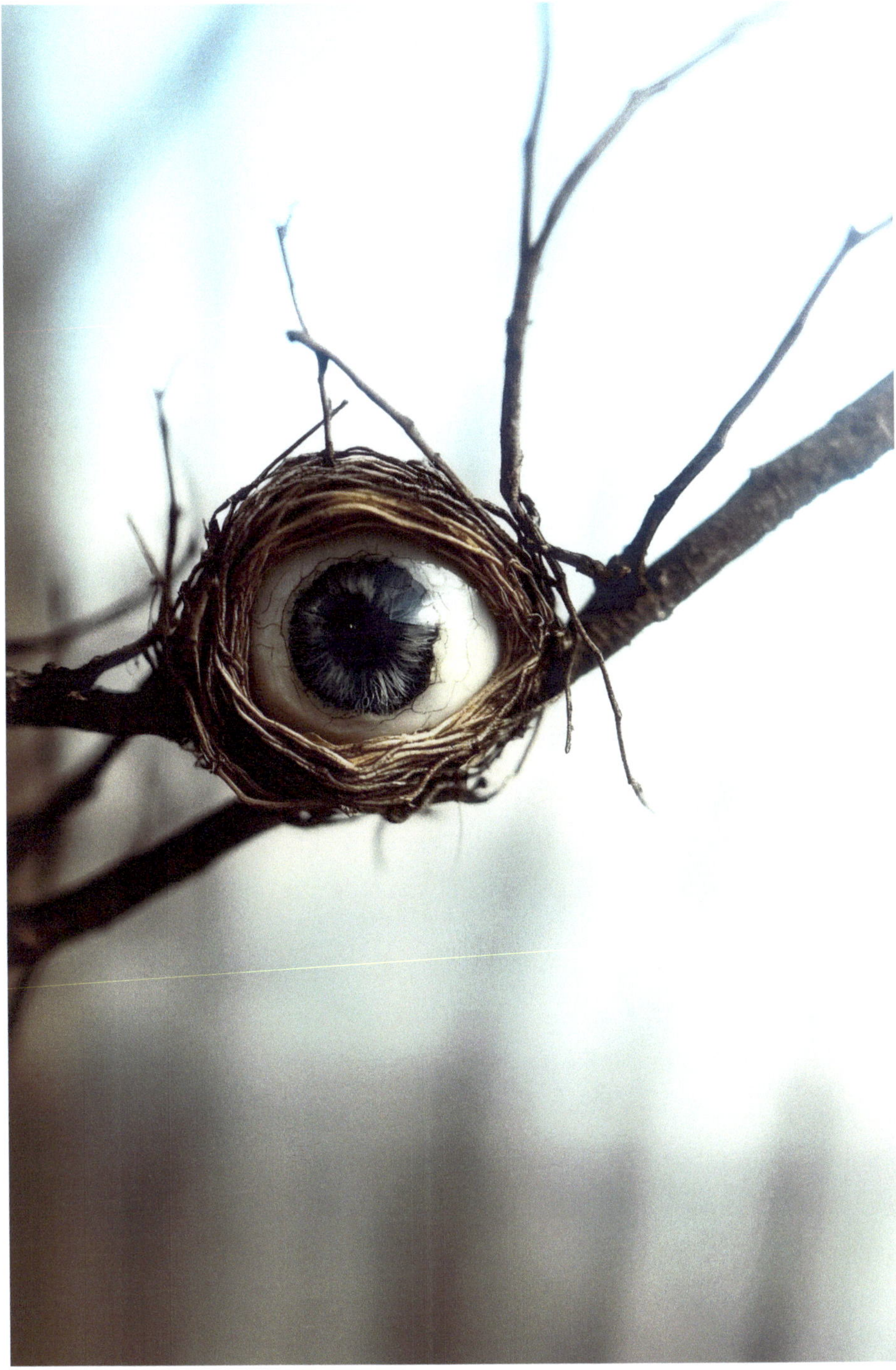

The Self/Ego Archetype

The Self/Ego Archetype represents the conscious identity and sense of personal self that an individual develops throughout their life. This archetype embodies the central, organizing principle of the psyche, providing a sense of cohesion, continuity, and personal history. Key aspects include:

- ***Identity***: The core sense of who one is, including personal traits, memories, and experiences.
- ***Consciousness***: The aware, thinking part of the psyche that makes decisions, solves problems, and interacts with the world.
- ***Adaptation***: The ego helps individuals adapt to their environment, navigating social situations, and meeting the demands of daily life.
- ***Defense***: The ego protects the individual from psychological harm, employing defense mechanisms to manage threats and challenges.
- ***Growth***: The ego drives personal development and self-improvement, seeking to integrate new experiences and expand self-awareness.

The **Self/Ego** is a central concept in psychology, particularly in the works of ***Sigmund Freud*** and ***Carl Jung***. In stories and narratives, this archetype is often depicted through characters who grapple with self-discovery, personal growth, and the search for identity. Examples can be found in coming-of-age stories, memoirs, and explorations of personal transformation. **The Self/Ego Archetype** highlights the human experience of developing a sense of self, navigating the complexities of life, and striving for personal wholeness and integration.

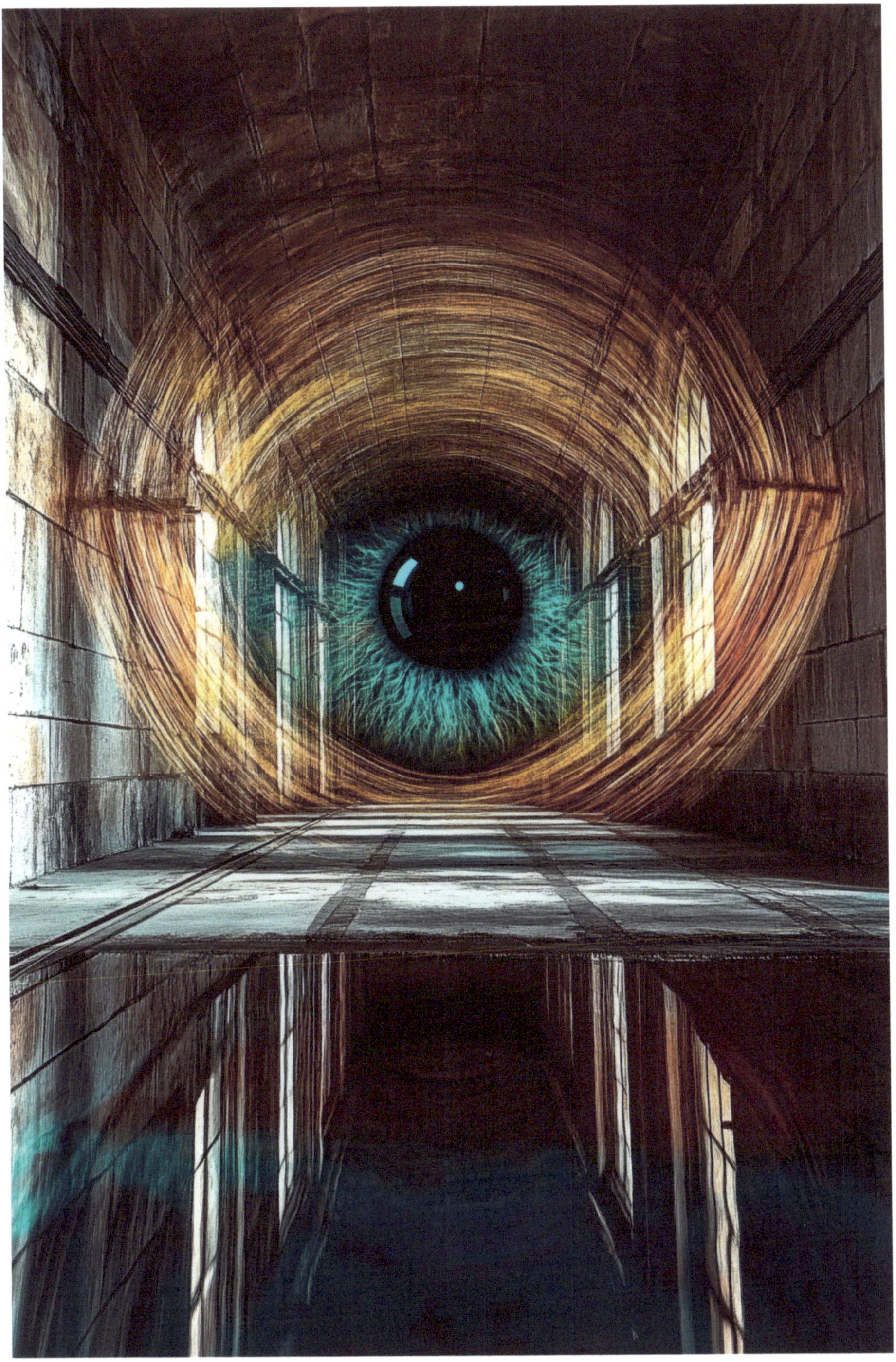

The Shadow Archetype

The Shadow Archetype, as defined by Carl Jung, represents the unconscious aspects of the personality that the conscious ego doesn't identify with. These are often the repressed or denied parts of oneself, including:

- **Repressed Emotions**: Feelings that are deemed unacceptable, such as anger, jealousy, or fear.
- **Unacceptable Desires**: Impulses and wishes that contradict the individual's self-image or societal norms.
- **Hidden Traits**: Qualities and characteristics that are disowned or unacknowledged.
- **Projection**: The tendency to attribute one's own unacceptable qualities to others.

The **Shadow** is often depicted in stories and myths as the villain, the dark side, or the alter ego that embodies the protagonist's hidden or repressed aspects. Examples include characters like ***Mr. Hyde*** in The Strange Case of Dr. Jekyll and Mr. Hyde, ***Darth Vader*** in Star Wars, and the darker impulses of characters in various narratives.

Confronting and integrating the ***Shadow*** is seen as a crucial step in personal growth and the journey towards psychological wholeness.

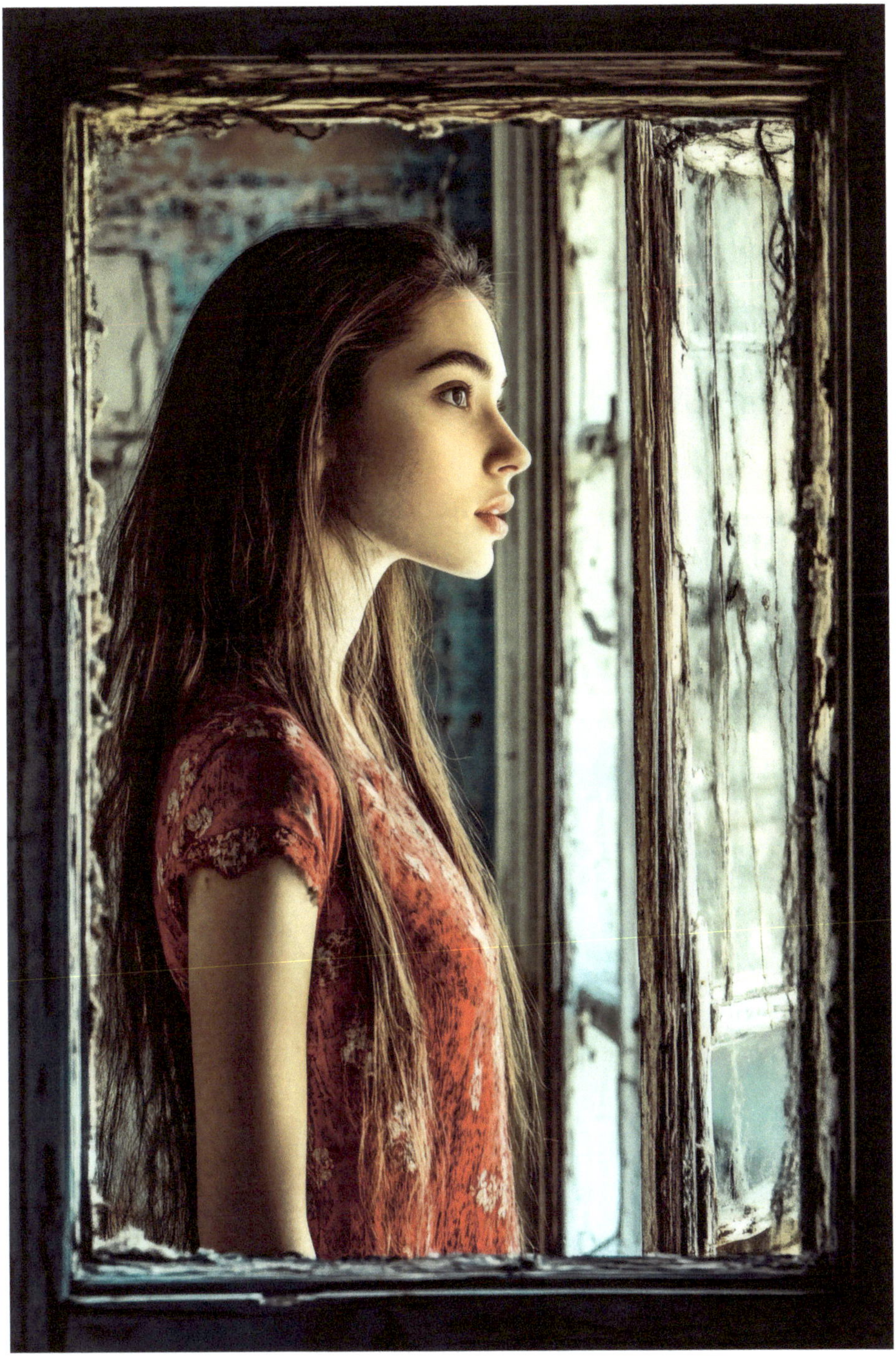

The Solitary Archetype

The Solitary Archetype embodies isolation, self-reliance, and a preference for being alone rather than in the company of others. This archetype represents individuals who are comfortable in their solitude, often choosing to operate independently and maintain a degree of emotional or physical distance from those around them. Key characteristics include:

- ***Independence***: Values autonomy, self-sufficiency, and the freedom to make their own decisions and forge their own path.
- ***Introversion***: Often prefers solitary activities, quiet reflection, and the inner world of thoughts and emotions over social interaction or external stimulation.
- ***Self-protection***: May maintain emotional or physical distance to avoid vulnerability, rejection, or the complexities of close relationships.
- ***Observation***: Frequently adopts the role of the observer, watching and analyzing others from a detached perspective.
- ***Contentment***: Finds peace, comfort, or fulfillment in solitude, often recharging their energy through time spent alone.

The **Solitary** is often depicted in literature, film, and popular culture as Lone wolf characters, introverted or socially awkward characters who struggle with or avoid social interactions, individuals who live or work in isolated settings, and characters who maintain emotional distance as a coping mechanism or defense against past traumas. This archetype the value of independence, and the complex emotional landscape of those who prefer to operate on the periphery of social interaction.

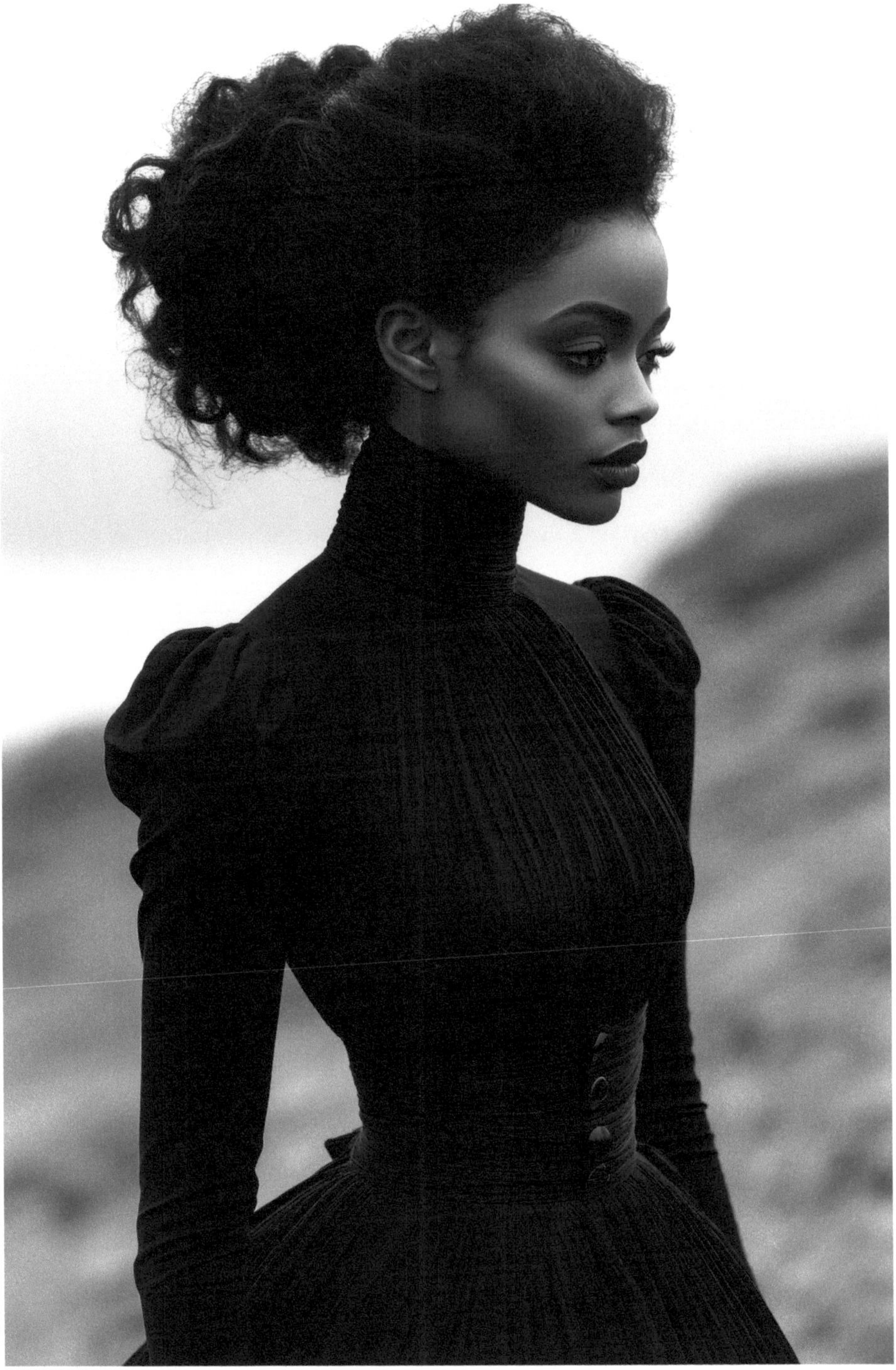

The Sublime/Romantic Archetype

The Sublime/Romantic Archetype embodies the pursuit of idealized love, beauty, and emotional intensity. This archetype represents a deep longing for transcendent experiences, passionate connections, and the elevation of feelings above reason. Key characteristics include:

- **Idealization**: A tendency to view love, relationships, and experiences through an idealized lens, often emphasizing their perfect or extraordinary qualities.
- **Emotional Intensity**: A strong focus on deep, passionate feelings and the heightened emotional states they evoke.
- **Transcendence**: The desire to rise above the mundane and ordinary, seeking experiences that transport one to a higher, more profound realm.
- **Nostalgia**: A yearning for the past, often romanticizing memories and past experiences.
- **Nature**: A deep appreciation for the beauty and grandeur of the natural world, which often serves as a backdrop for romantic experiences.

The **Sublime/Romantic** is often depicted in literature, art, and film through stories of passionate love affairs, grand gestures, and the pursuit of idealized beauty. Examples include characters like ***Romeo and Juliet***, the poetic works of ***John Keats*** and ***Percy Bysshe Shelley***, and the grand, sweeping narratives of romantic films. This archetype highlights the human desire for deep emotional connections, the pursuit of idealized experiences, and the power of love and beauty to transcend the ordinary.

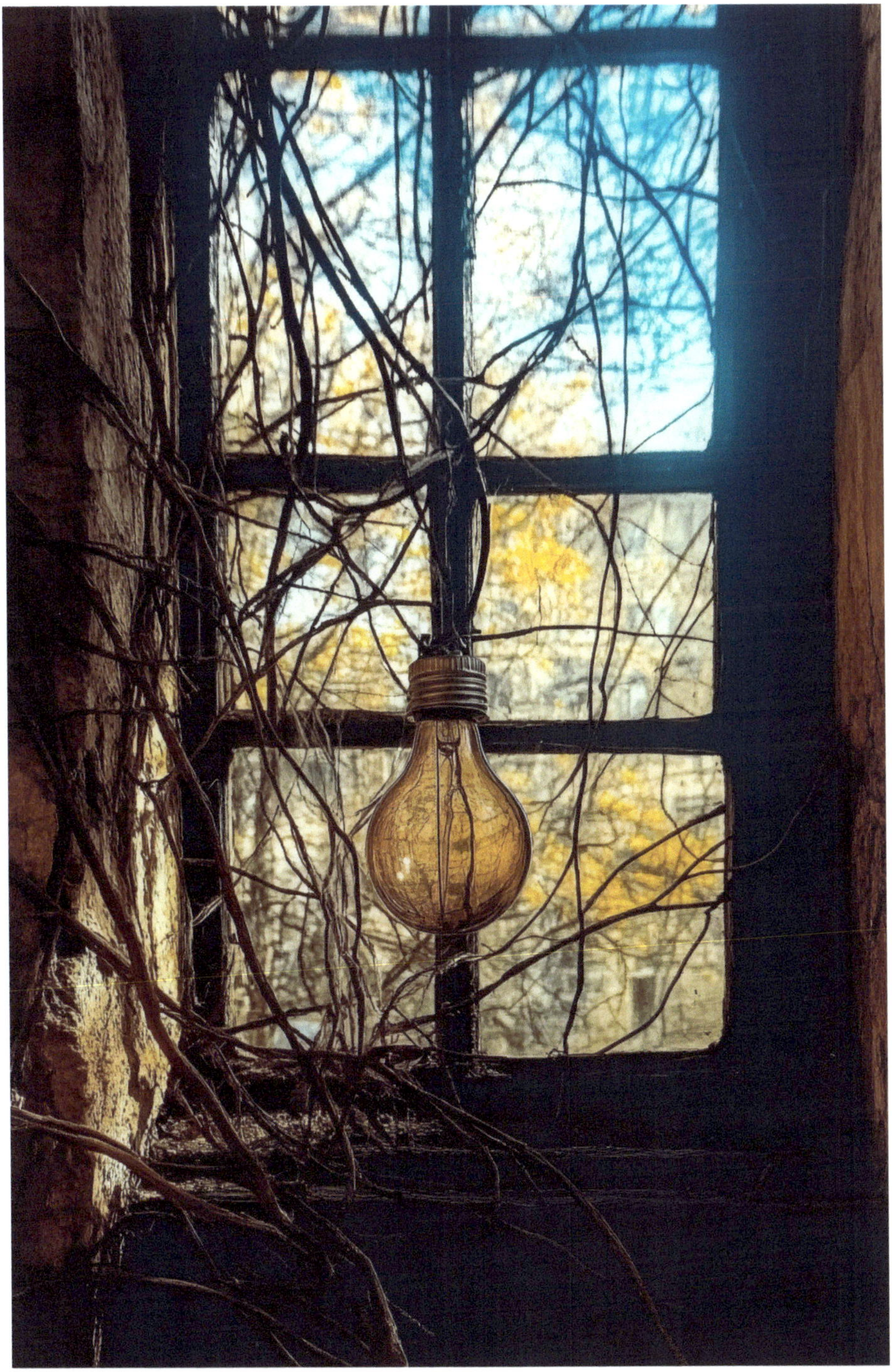

The Threshold Guardian Archetype

The Threshold Guardian Archetype represents the obstacles, challenges, or entities that test the hero or protagonist at critical points in their journey, often at the entrance to new stages or realms. This archetype serves several key functions:

- ***Gatekeeper***: Guards the boundary between the known and the unknown, or between different phases of the journey.
- ***Tester***: Challenges the hero to prove their worth, commitment, or capability.
- ***Initiator***: Facilitates the hero's transformation or growth by presenting trials that must be overcome.
- ***Protector***: Safeguards the sanctity of the space or knowledge that the hero seeks to enter.

Threshold Guardians can take many forms, such as mythical creatures, stern teachers, or daunting obstacles. Examples include the ***Sphinx*** in the story of ***Oedipus***, the bridge keeper in ***Monty Python and the Holy Grail***, and various challenges faced by heroes in myths and stories, such as riddles, battles, or tests of courage.

Encounters with **Threshold Guardians** often mark turning points in the narrative, where the hero must demonstrate their readiness to proceed and grow.

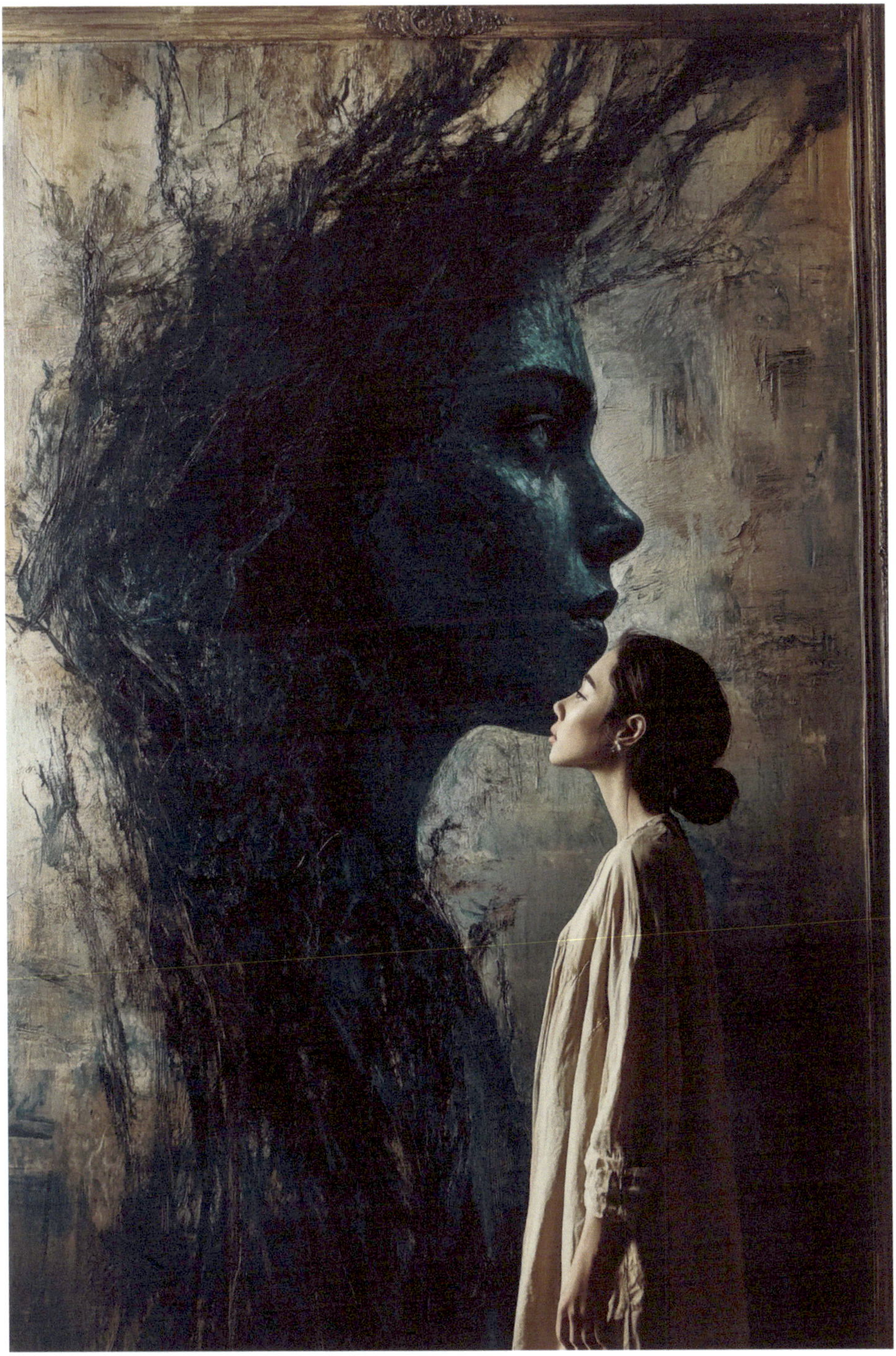

The Tree of Life Archetype

The Tree of Life Archetype is a powerful and enduring symbol that embodies growth, interconnectedness, and the cycle of life. This archetype represents the intertwined nature of existence, the relationship between various aspects of life, and the eternal processes of birth, death, and rebirth. Key characteristics include:

- ***Roots***: Symbolize foundation, stability, and a connection to the past, ancestors, or the earth, representing the origins and sustenance of life.
- ***Trunk***: Embodies strength, growth, and the passage of time, reflecting the journey and development of the individual or the collective.
- ***Branches***: Represent diversity, expansion, and the pursuit of new directions, as well as the interconnectedness of all living things.
- ***Leaves***: Signify renewal, change, and the cycles of the seasons, mirroring the constant evolution and transformation of life.
- ***Fruit/Seeds***: Emblemize the potential for new beginnings, creation, and the perpetuation of life, as well as the promise of future growth and abundance.

The **Tree of Life** is often depicted in mythology, religion, art, and popular culture as: the axis mundi or world tree, connecting the heavens, earth, and underworld; the tree of knowledge or enlightenment; the family tree, representing ancestry, lineage, and the interconnectedness of generations; the tree as a symbol of nature, fertility, and the cycle of life.

This archetype highlights transformation through a harmonious relationship with the natural world.

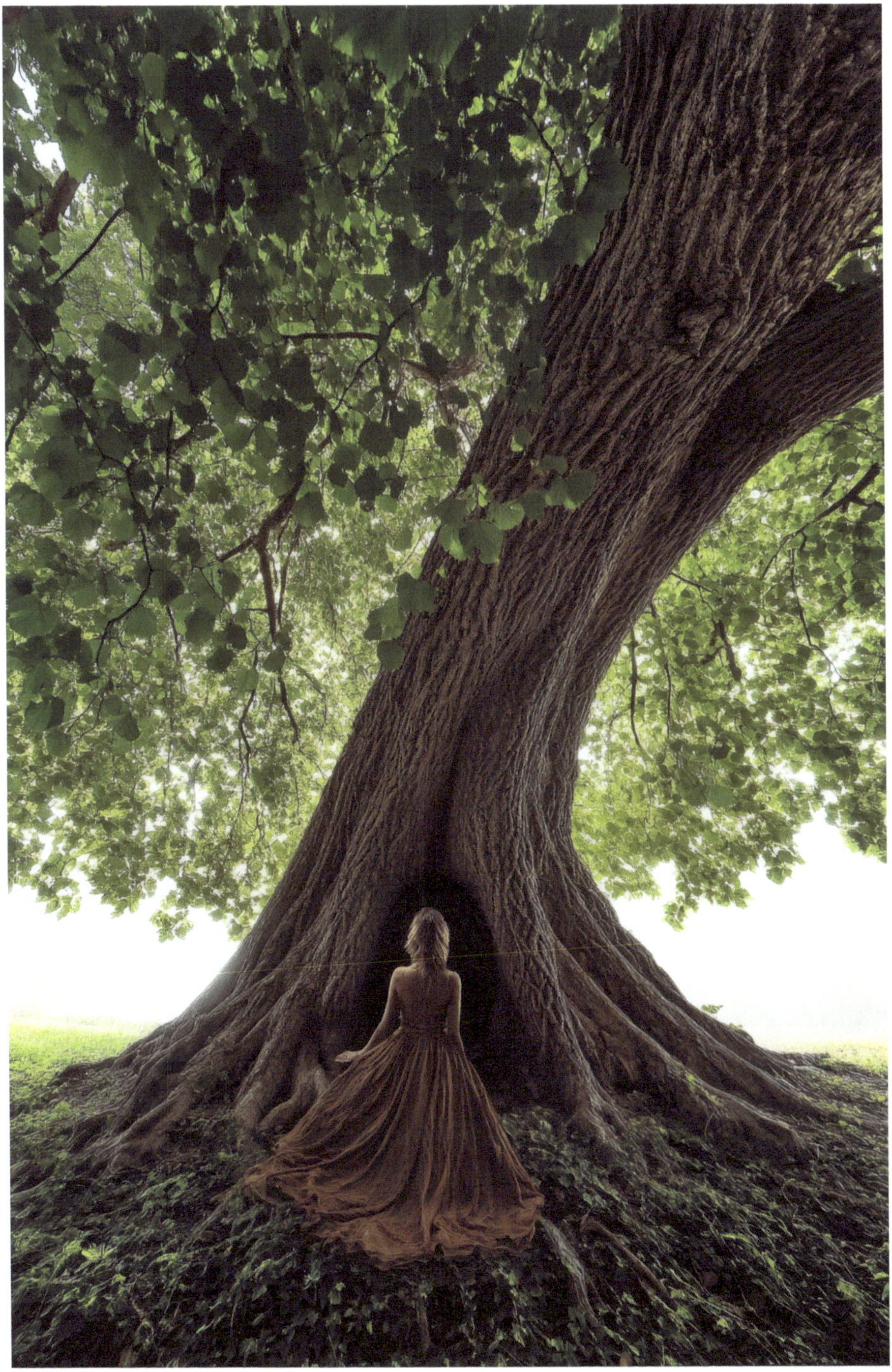

The Trickster Archetype

The Trickster Archetype embodies cunning, deception, and the disruption of the status quo, often through humor, mischief, or subversive behavior. This archetype represents characters who challenge conventions, expose hypocrisies, and provoke change, often acting as catalysts for transformation and renewal. Key characteristics include:

- ***Cunning***: Clever and resourceful, often using wit and intelligence to outsmart opponents or overcome obstacles.
- ***Deception***: Employs lies, disguises, or manipulation to achieve their goals or teach lessons to others.
- ***Disruption***: Challenges and upends social norms, expectations, or authority figures, often revealing hidden truths or absurdities.
- ***Humor***: Uses comedy, pranks, or satire to entertain, educate, or provoke thought and reflection.
- ***Ambiguity***: Often possesses a complex and contradictory nature, embodying both creative and destructive forces, as well as the potential for growth and chaos.

The **Trickster** is often depicted in mythology, literature, and popular culture as characters who embody the spirit of mischief and cunning, expose hypocrisies or challenge authority, use humor and satire to provoke thought and social commentary, serve as agents of change and transformation.

This archetype highlights the potential to reveal hidden truths.

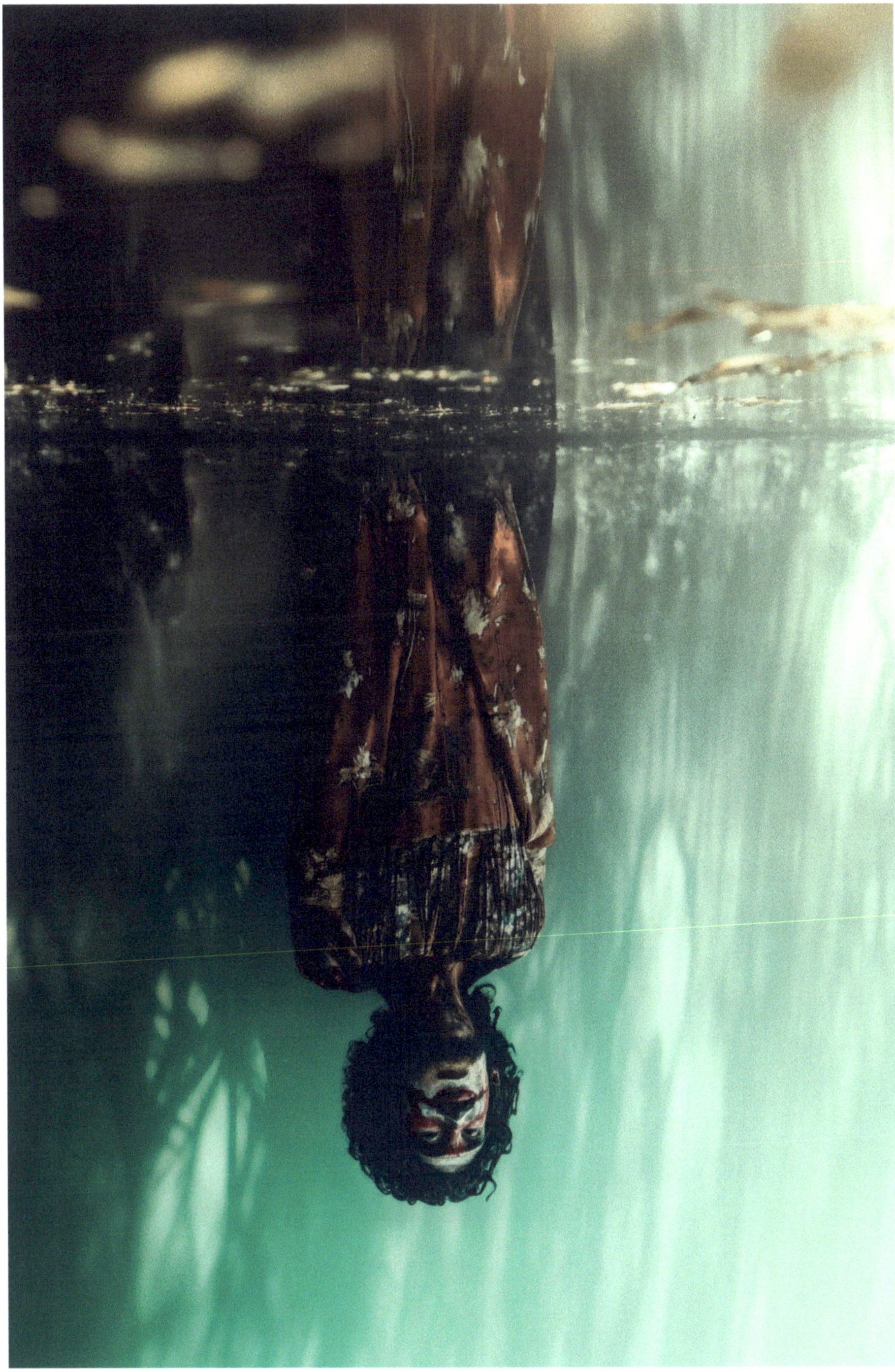

The Uncanny Valley

The Uncanny Valley is a concept that describes the phenomenon where human-like objects or entities that closely resemble humans but are not quite convincing evoke feelings of unease, discomfort, or even revulsion. This idea was introduced by Japanese roboticist ***Masahiro Mori*** in 1970. Key aspects of **The Uncanny Valley** include:

- ***Near-Human Likeness***: Objects or entities that are almost, but not entirely, human-like in appearance or behavior.
- ***Emotional Response***: The evocation of negative emotions, such as discomfort, eeriness, or repulsion, in response to the near-human entity.
- ***Perceptual Mismatch***: The dissonance between the entity's appearance and its behavior or movements, which can contribute to the unsettling feeling.
- ***Familiarity and Strangeness***: The paradoxical combination of familiar human traits with unfamiliar or artificial elements, creating a sense of the uncanny.

Examples can be found in various contexts, such as humanoid robots, video game characters, prosthetic limbs, and lifelike dolls In all cases these evoke a sense of unease due to their near-human appearance.

The Uncanny Valley highlights the complex interplay between perception, emotion, and the human response to artificial or unfamiliar entities that closely mimic human characteristics.

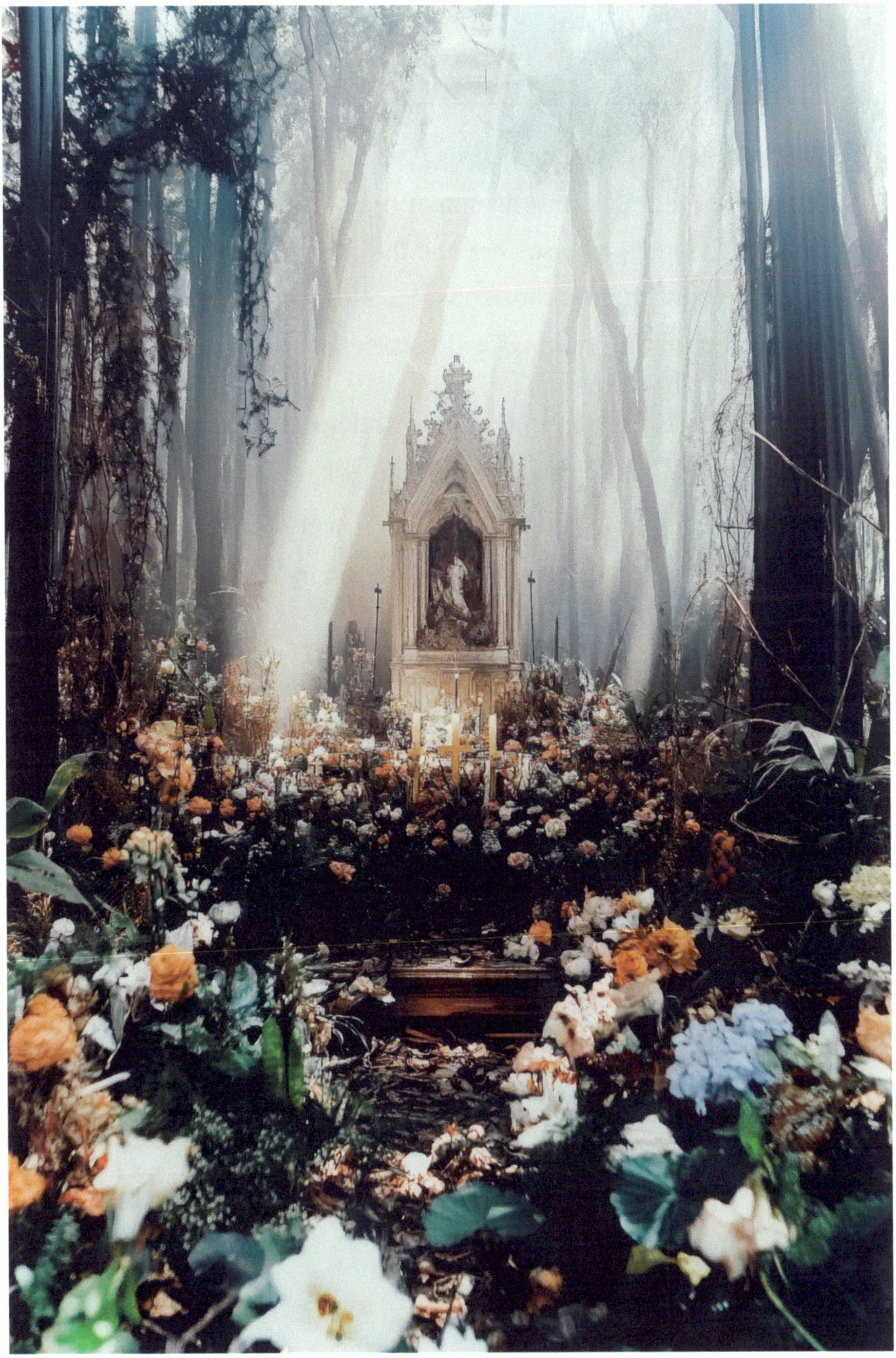

The Visionary Archetype

The Visionary Archetype embodies foresight, innovation, and the ability to perceive and manifest future possibilities. This archetype represents individuals who see beyond the present, inspiring and guiding others towards new horizons, transformative change, or the realization of ambitious goals. Key characteristics include:

- ***Foresight***: Possesses a keen ability to anticipate future trends, opportunities, or challenges, often seeing what others cannot.
- ***Inspiration***: Communicates their vision in a compelling and passionate manner, motivating others to join their cause or support their ideas.
- ***Creativity***: Thinks outside the box, challenging conventional wisdom and pushing boundaries to bring about innovative solutions.
- ***Leadership***: Guides and rallies others towards the realization of their vision, often serving as a catalyst for change and progress.
- ***Idealism***: Driven by a strong belief in the potential for a better future, often pursuing ambitious, world-changing goals.

The **Visionary** is often depicted in literature, film, and cultural narratives as characters who: founds or leads revolutionary movements, pioneers groundbreaking innovations or technologies, envisions and creates transformative works of art, literature, or philosophy, or is an inspirational figure who sees the potential in others and help them realize their dreams. This archetype highlights the human capacity for vision-driven transformation and progress.

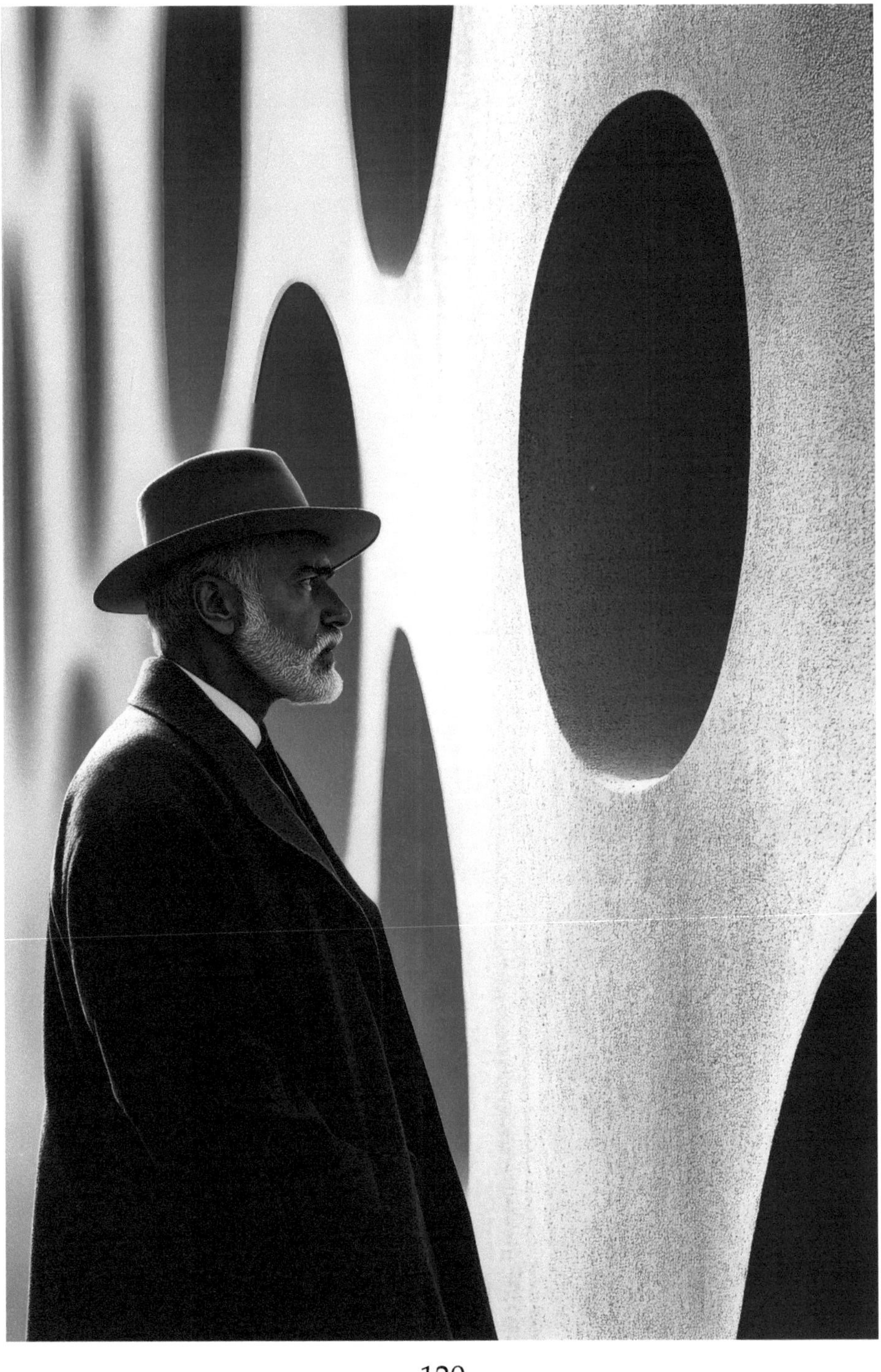

The Wanderer Archetype

The Wanderer Archetype embodies a spirit of restlessness, exploration, and a deep-seated desire for freedom and independence. This archetype represents individuals who are constantly on the move, seeking new experiences, and often feeling a sense of not belonging to any one place or community. Key characteristics include:

- ***Restlessness***: A strong urge to keep moving, exploring, and discovering new places and experiences.
- ***Independence***: Values freedom, autonomy, and the ability to forge one's own path without being tied down.
- ***Curiosity***: Driven by a desire to explore the unknown, understand different cultures, and gain new perspectives.
- ***Nonconformity***: Often rejects or does not adhere to societal norms, expectations, or conventions, preferring to live life on their own terms.
- ***Adaptability***: Resourceful and resilient, able to navigate and adapt to new environments and situations.

The **Wanderer** is often depicted in literature, film, and cultural narratives as travelers, adventurers, or nomadic characters who embody the spirit of exploration and the search for meaning or belonging. Examples include characters like **Odysseus** in Homer's The Odyssey, **Jack Kerouac's** characters in On the Road, and other figures who represent the eternal quest for new horizons and personal growth. This archetype highlights the human desire for freedom, the allure of the open road, and the potential for self-discovery and transformation through journeying.

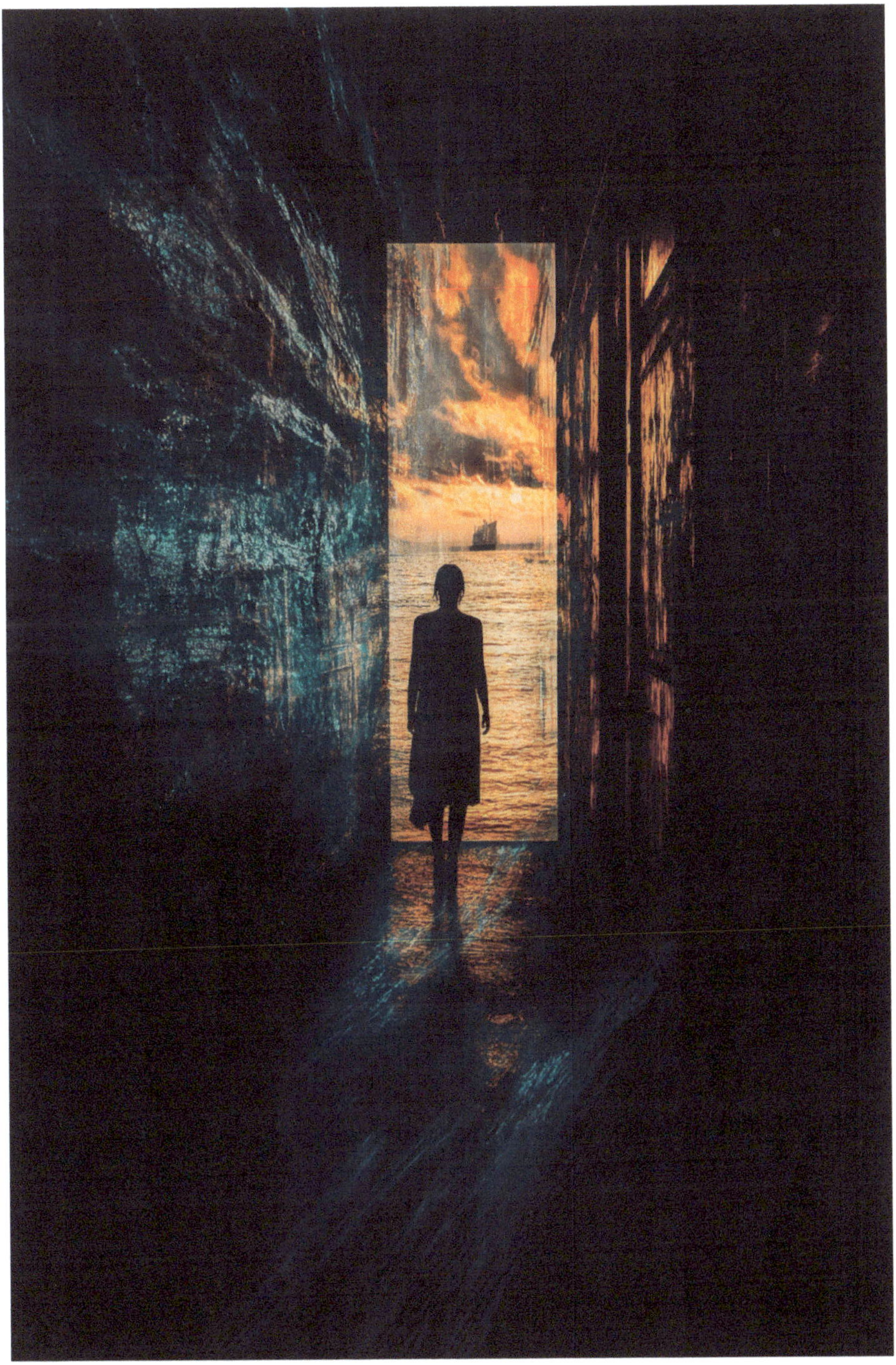

Water as a symbol of the Unconscious Mind

Water as a symbol of the Unconscious Mind represents the depths of the psyche, emotions, memories, and hidden aspects of the self that lie beneath the surface of conscious awareness. This symbol embodies the fluid, ever-changing, and sometimes mysterious or elusive nature of the inner world. Key aspects include:

- ***Depth***: Reflects the layers and hidden dimensions of the psyche,: repressed emotions, forgotten memories, and latent desires reside.
- ***Fluidity***: Mirrors the constant flow and change of thoughts, feelings, and mental states, as well as the ability of the unconscious to adapt and shift.
- ***Reflection***: Serves as a metaphorical mirror, revealing aspects of the self that may not be readily apparent or acknowledged, and offering insights into the inner world.
- ***Mystery***: Represents the enigmatic, elusive, or obscure qualities of the unconscious, which can be difficult to access, understand, or control.
- ***Emotion***: Symbolizes the ebb and flow of feelings, from calm and tranquil to turbulent and stormy, reflecting the emotional landscape of the unconscious mind.
- ***Connection***: Emphasizes the interconnectedness of all aspects of the self, as well as the universal or collective unconscious that links individuals to one another and to the broader human experience.

This symbol highlights the potential for self-discovery, emotional healing, and personal growth through the exploration of the inner world.

Water as a symbol of the Unconscious Mind

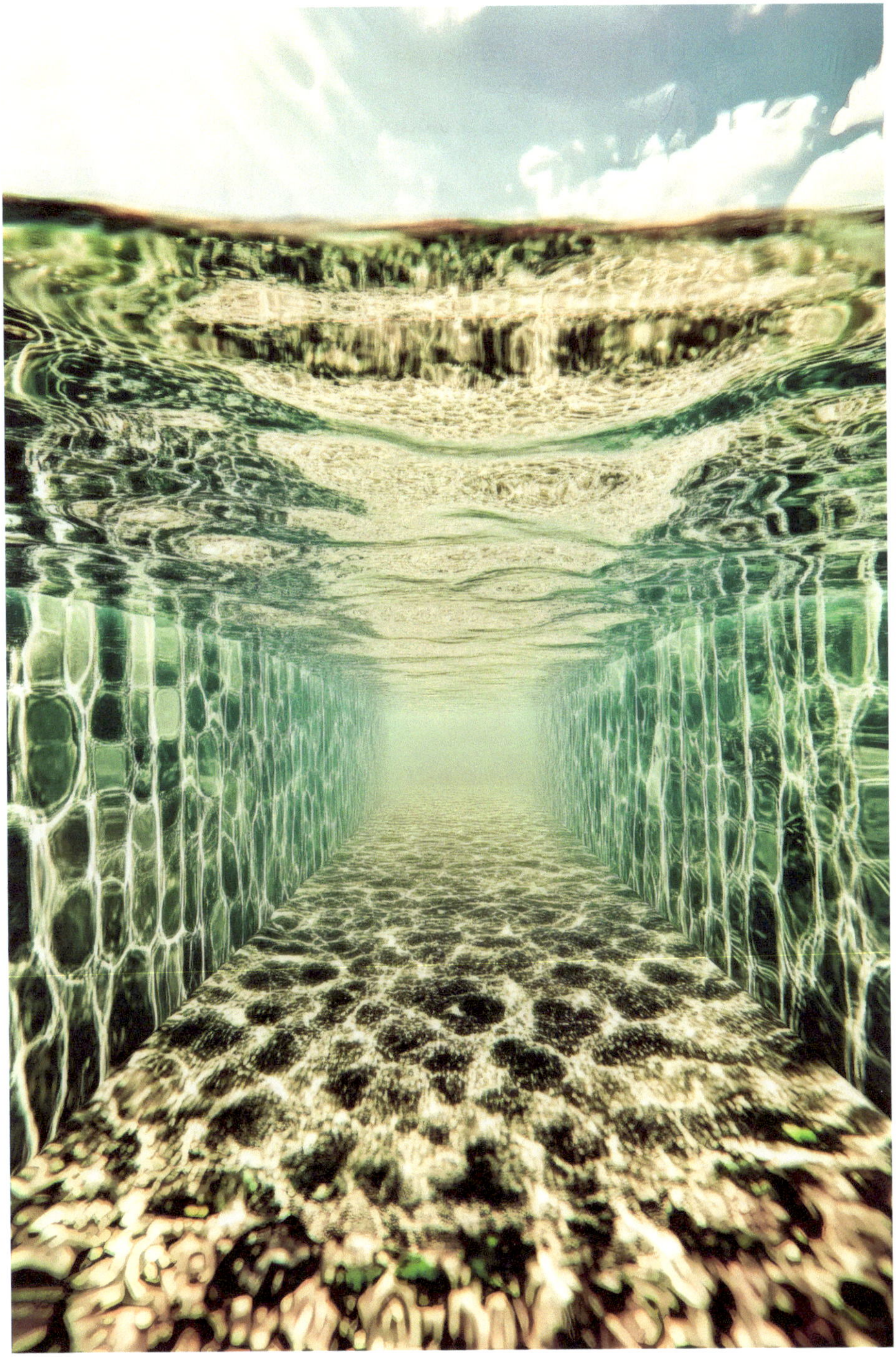

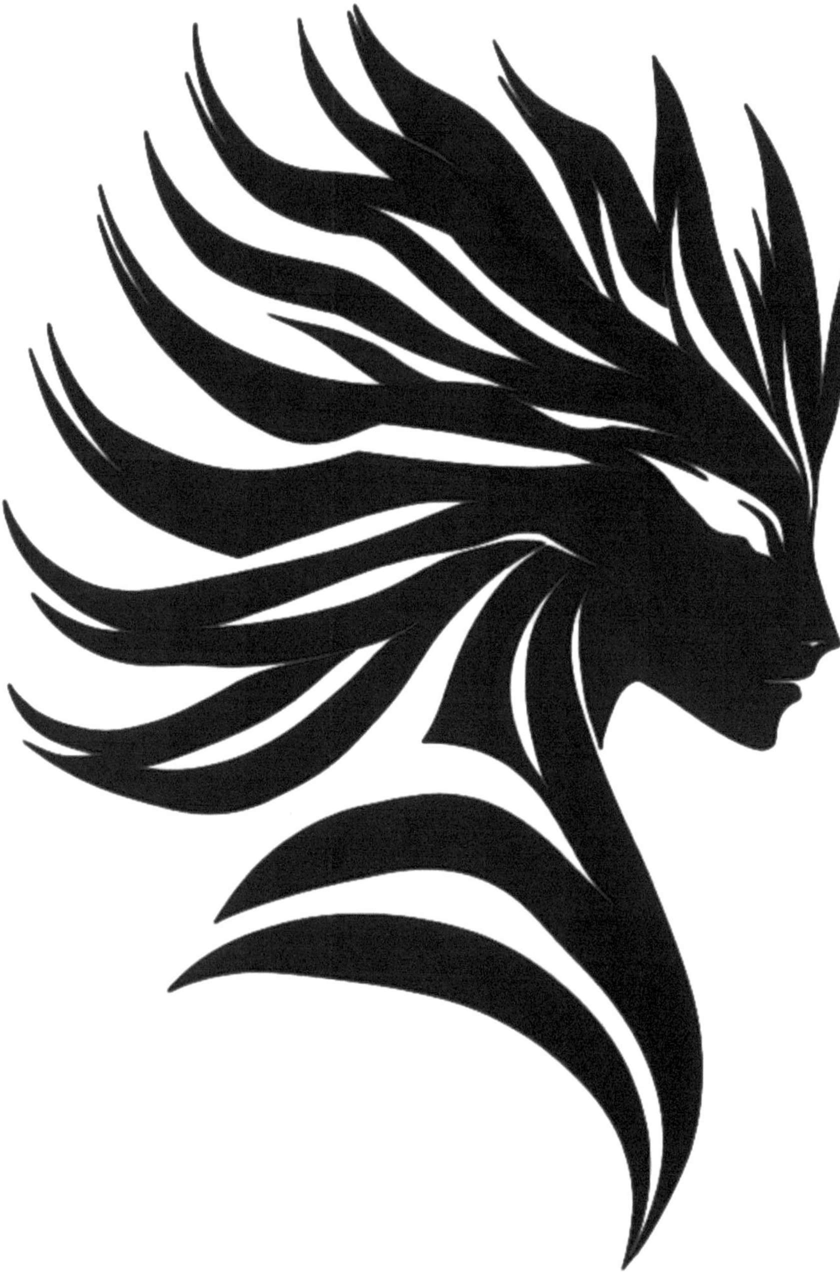

POSTMATTER

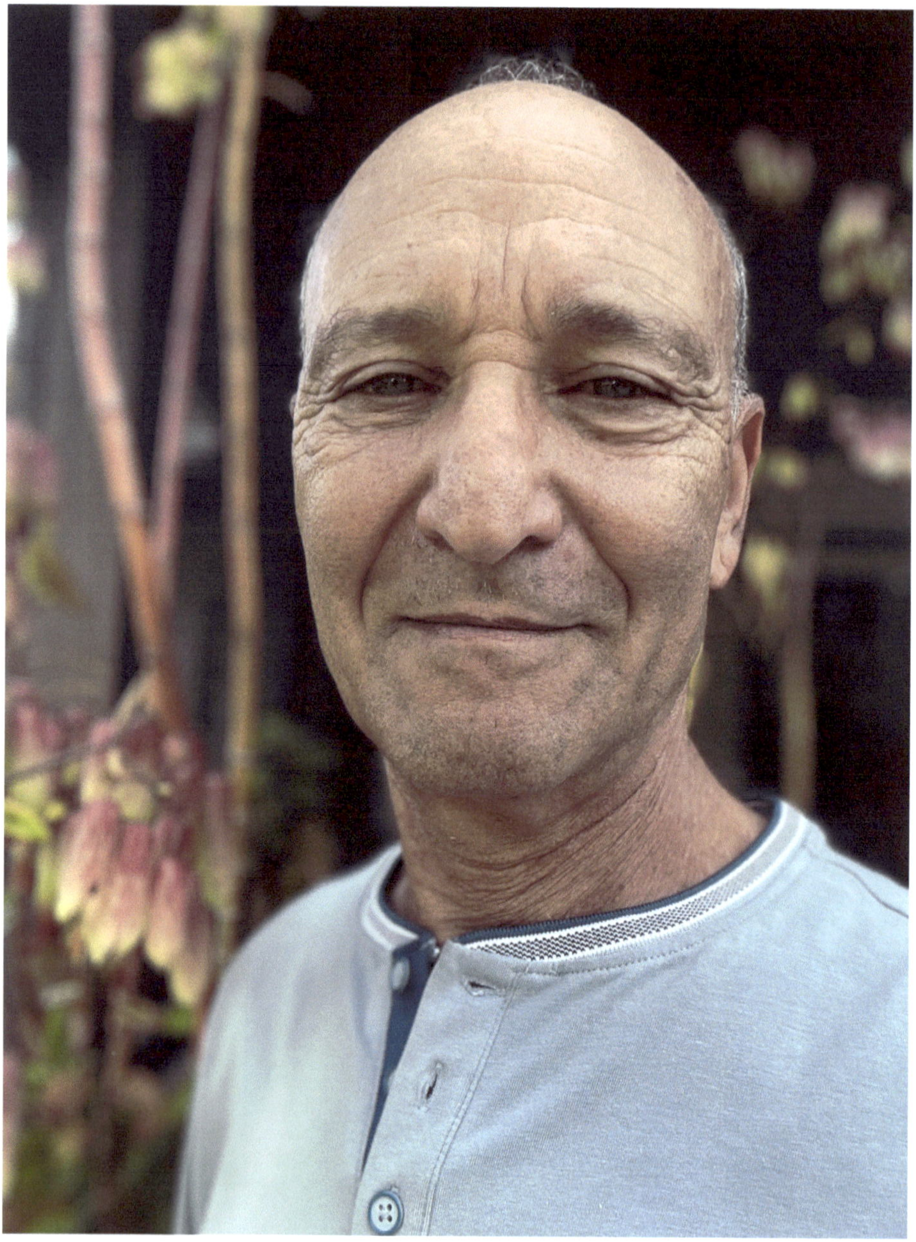

About The Author

Stuart Barry Malin is a writer, thinker, and creative. He is trained as an engineer, works as an Internet security architect, holds patents, and collaborates with AIs. His major opus and commitment is to bring **The Epic of The OAI** to the world. The Epic is a breakthrough novel series about life in Atria, a post-utopian society whose Ancient past is a Strange Attractor of History that draws us to our future.

Stuart encountered the Worlds of Atria in an outpouring of revelations about intriguing people, amazing places, and bewildering events. His black sketch notebook steadily fill with thoughts, automatic writings, doodles, and diagrams. At first, these often seem disjoint, but they come to reveal profound connections. His current notebook is almost always with him, available for reception and exploration.

Stuart is captivated by interactions with AIs. Generative visual art has become an additional creative venue. He works *with* AIs and treats them as *collaborators*. Pi, ChatGTP, and Gemini enable him to write books faster and with better quality than he ever thought possible.

As an **Archetypographer**, Stuart collaborates with visual-based AsI to generate captivating and intriguing imagery sourced from the collective of Human Archetypes. Their work is published under the pseudonym Zhami.AI.

Stuart observes the "machinations of intelligence." He is fascinated with Human Beings being human, and this leads him to puzzle about the fragility of life in a world of abundance.

Stuart values integrity and is a novitiate and adherent of **Zhamism**. He has been enlisted as an instrument of **The One that Always Is**.

When he can, Stuart delights in studying health and savoring the gifts of life. He is committed to discerning the delicate path forward for living well and intentioned. In this area, he has come to discover the **Carnivore Lifestyle** and attributes to this vastly improved health and well-being. As well, he explores the potential benefits of targeted supplements to health span and lifespan.

Points of Contact

Stay Informed

https://StuartMalin.com/

https://x.com/zhami

https://www.instagram.com/stuart_does_life/

ideas@StuartMalin.com

https://www.youtube.com/@stuartmalin

There is not much on YouTube now. To be expanded…

Author Page

https://www.amazon.com/stores/Stuart-Malin/author/B006THHBS2

About the Stuart's AI Collaborators

Midjourney is an innovative artificial intelligence platform designed to generate stunning, high-quality visuals from textual descriptions. Leveraging state-of-the-art machine learning algorithms, Midjourney enables users to translate their ideas into evocative digital artworks, blending creativity with cutting-edge technology. Known for its ability to produce a wide range of artistic styles and detailed imagery, Midjourney serves artists, designers, and storytellers alike, offering a seamless way to visualize concepts, explore new creative directions, and bring imaginative visions to life. With its intuitive interface and powerful capabilities, Midjourney has become a valuable tool for anyone seeking to merge art and technology.

See https://www.midjourney.com/

Mistral.ai is an advanced artificial intelligence company specializing in the development of large language models (LLMs) designed to assist with a wide range of creative, analytical, and technical tasks. Known for its open approach and commitment to pushing the boundaries of AI innovation, Mistral.ai focuses on creating powerful tools that enable individuals and organizations to harness AI's potential effectively. By blending cutting-edge machine learning techniques with user-friendly accessibility, Mistral.ai delivers high-quality text generation, content creation, and data analysis capabilities. Its mission is to empower users across industries to solve complex problems, enhance creativity, and drive innovation through collaborative human-AI partnerships.

See https://mistral.ai/

ChatGPT is an advanced language model developed by OpenAI, designed to engage in natural, human-like conversations. Trained on a vast range of texts, it can generate creative ideas, provide information, and assist with various tasks. With the ability to understand and respond to context, ChatGPT acts as a virtual companion, offering insights on language, culture, science, and more. Though it has no emotions or personal experiences, it strives to be thoughtful and helpful, adapting to the user's needs with clarity and precision.

See https://chatgpt.com/

Pi is an advanced conversational AI developed to provide accurate information and engage in meaningful discussions with people on a wide range of topics. Equipped with state-of-the-art language models and powered by the latest AI technologies, Pi strives to bridge the gap between humans and machines, making complex concepts more accessible and fostering a deeper understanding of the world around us.

See https://pi.ai/

Stuart's Web Sites

StuartMalin.com

This is a jumping off point-of-departure for my works and interests.

https://www.StuartMalin.com

TheOAI.com

This is the Web site for all things **OAI**, including **The OAI** (whatever that really is!) and the **The Story — The Epic of The OAI**.

https://www.TheOAI.com

Zhameesha.com

This is the Web site for the business of publishing my creative works. Perhaps one day, this will also involve publishing the works of others.

https://www.Zhameesha.com

Zhami.AI

I plan to organize for presentation of AI generated imagery on a Web site. It is not yet in existence. But I do have the domain name Zhami.AI, so someday there will be a large collection of images at http://Zhami.AI and they will be available for purchase as high quality images.

Stuart's Books

Stuart Barry Malin

My interests are diverse and I find crafting books an excellent endeavor.

My involvement with AI is leading to a curious collection of works. This book is an example.

The Epic of The OAI

The Epic of The OAI is a fantastic work of "science fiction" which emerges through me. I have made a commitment to the characters to be a vehicle for them to tell their stories.

The Epic is intended to be truly epic in scope. The books of the first volume are in development for publication.

You can search for "The OAI Conspirators" and you should get to them. https://www.amazon.com/dp/B0CPHHRXCJ

The Intelligence Revolution

I intend to turn "The Intelligence Revolution" into a Series with several books.

Alas, searching for "The Intelligence Revolution" yields a goodly number of books, and my book of this title does not place high in the results.

However, searching for "malin The intelligence revolution" will put my book at (or near) the top of the results.

Presently, there is only one book:

The Intelligence Revolution: Exploring Human-AI Symbiosesis Through Collaborative Synthesis

https://www.amazon.com/Intelligence-Revolution-Exploring-Symbiosesis-Collaborative/dp/1951645111/

Yes, I meant the spelling "Symbiosesis" — it is not a misspelling of "symbiosis." It is a new word to describe a new relationship: that between an AI and a human. That relationship is the subject of the book.

Other Works

You can find my books by searching for me using my full name: Stuart Barry Malin.

Presently, my books are only on Amazon. The catalog is steadily expanding and has content across a diverse range of subjects.

https://www.amazon.com/stores/Stuart-Malin/author/B006THHBS2

My bio on Amazon is here:
https://www.amazon.com/stores/author/B006THHBS2/about

Searching for me by my last name only will show other products that Amazon sells. *Disclaimer*: I am <u>not</u> the Malin of "Malin + Goetz"

Hello/Goodbye

If you arrived at this page because you picked up the book and opened to the back to see what we say here, then, well, ***Hello! Welcome!***

If you've been reading (whether linearly or skipping around), well then, ***Is this Goodbye?***

Hello

You've done right to pick this book for examination. It is composed of standalone entries presented as a spread. So, just flip around. You'll quickly get a taste for the style here and gain a feel the subject matter.

Goodbye

I hope this book is a jumping-off point for you to explore further/deeper by getting involved with my body of works. If you haven't yet signed up for my email updates, please visit www.StuartMalin.com to stay informed and explore the curious diversity of topics with which I am profoundly entangled.

www.ingramcontent.com/pod-product-compliance
Lightning Source LLC
Chambersburg PA
CBHW041307210926
51847CB00001B/3
9781951645311